CAMPAIGN 383

BEREZINA 1812

Napoleon's Hollow Victory

ALEXANDER MIKABERIDZE ILLUSTRATED BY ADAM HOOK

Series editor Nikolai Bogdanovic

OSPREY PUBLISHING
Bloomsbury Publishing Plc
Kemp House, Chawley Park, Cumnor Hill, Oxford OX2 9PH, UK
29 Earlsfort Terrace, Dublin 2, Ireland
1385 Broadway, 5th Floor, New York, NY 10018, USA
E-mail: info@ospreypublishing.com
www.ospreypublishing.com

OSPREY is a trademark of Osprey Publishing Ltd

First published in Great Britain in 2022

A catalogue record for this book is available from the British Library.

ISBN: PB 9781472850188; eBook 9781472850171; ePDF 9781472850164; XML 9781472850195

22 23 24 25 26 10 9 8 7 6 5 4 3 2 1

Maps by Bounford.com
3D BEVs by Paul Kime
Index by Alison Worthington
Typeset by PDQ Digital Media Solutions, Bungay, UK
Printed and bound in India by Replika Press Private Ltd.

Key to military symbols

XXXXX Army Group · XXXX Army · XXX Corps · XX Division · X Brigade · III Regiment · II Battalion · I Company/Battery · Infantry · Artillery · Cavalry · Unit HQ · Engineer · Medical · Navy · Ordnance

Key to unit identification

Unit identifier · Parent unit · Commander · (+) with added elements · (–) less elements

Artist's note

Readers may care to note that the original paintings from which the colour plates in this book were prepared are available for private sale. All reproduction copyright whatsoever is retained by the publishers. All enquiries should be addressed to:

Scorpio, 158 Mill Road, Hailsham, East Sussex BN27 2SH, UK
Email: scorpiopaintings@btinternet.com

The publishers regret that they can enter into no correspondence upon this matter.

Author's note

This book is dedicated to Colonel Jason Musteen, a true warrior-scholar whose friendship, advice, and support I value greatly.

Osprey Publishing supports the Woodland Trust, the UK's leading woodland conservation charity.

To find out more about our authors and books visit **www.ospreypublishing.com**. Here you will find extracts, author interviews, details of forthcoming events and the option to sign up for our newsletter.

Front cover main image: The Charge of Doumerc's 'Men of Iron', 28 November 1812. (Adam Hook)

Title page image: A column of French and allied soldiers trudges through the desolate Russian landscape during Napoleon's retreat. (Leemage/Corbis via Getty Images)

CONTENTS

French and Russian forces on the eve of the war

ORIGINS OF THE CAMPAIGN

Standing on the hill overlooking the Nieman River, the boundary of the Russian Empire, was the familiar silhouette of the French emperor. It was 24 June 1812, a clear summer morning. The grand imperial army, which Napoleon had gathered for a war with Russia, was marching eastwards across pontoon bridges. 'Soldiers, Russia is swept away by her fate,' the Emperor had exhorted his troops in a proclamation. 'She places us between dishonour and war: the choice cannot be in doubt. Let us, then, march forward!'

The conflict between Russia and France did not come as a surprise to contemporaries, as the last few years had chilled the friendship between Napoleon and Emperor Alexander I of Russia that had been expressed effusively at Tilsit in July 1807. Each was disappointed and antagonized by the conduct of the other. For his part, Alexander remained disgruntled by military and diplomatic setbacks suffered at the hands of Napoleon and deeply concerned by his dominance over Europe. France's economic war with Britain (the so-called Continental System), which Alexander was obliged to join under the terms of Tilsit, proved disadvantageous as Russia lost lucrative trade with Britain, a major destination for wheat, timber, hemp, tallow and other resources. Without compensation for lost revenue, the Russian economy faced financial ruin.

Napoleon and his army crossing the Nieman River in 1812, an engraving by Paul Girardet. (Hulton Archive/ Getty Images)

The Russian emperor Alexander I, painted by George Dawe. Alexander (1777–1825) ascended to the throne after the murder of his father, Paul I. (Fine Art Images/Heritage Images/Getty Images)

More crucially, there was a profound misalignment of Russian and French interests on a range of geopolitical issues. The Polish Question deeply strained their relations. The old Kingdom of Poland had been partitioned and swallowed up by Russia, Prussia, and Austria between 1772 and 1795. Napoleon's creation of the Grand Duchy of Warsaw, 'a splinter in the body of Russia', as Alexander described it, awakened Russian fears of a full reconstitution of Polish lands and national identity. The czar requested a guarantee that Napoleon would not revive an independent Poland, but Napoleon refused to grant it. Then there was the fate of the Ottoman Empire, where the Russian ambition to acquire territory through conquest appeared to be a move that France was very determined to block. Similarly, Napoleon's reorganization of Germany affected princes who were related to the Romanov dynasty; Alexander's sister Catherine was married to the son and heir of the Duke of Oldenburg, and the French annexation of that principality in 1810 (in violation of guarantees given at Tilsit three years earlier) looked like a deliberate insult to the Russian potentate. Napoleon's marriage to the Habsburg princess Marie-Louise and the subsequent Franco-Austrian rapprochement was unwelcome in Russia and had set the two emperors at even greater variance.

It was soon apparent that the political arrangement that had been reached at Tilsit had outlived its usefulness. In March 1810, the French foreign minister argued that the alliance with Russia had run its course and that France should, therefore, return to its traditional reliance on the Ottoman Empire, Sweden and Poland to contain the 'Russian imperial colossus'. A month later, Napoleon approved a proposal for the creation of an alliance between France, Sweden, Denmark and the Grand Duchy of Warsaw, which, however, did not materialize due to Swedish and Danish reluctance to participate. At the same time, Czar Alexander and his advisors also reached the conclusion that war with France was imminent, and sought to entice Berlin and Vienna to turn against Napoleon. But the French presence in the Germanic states and the recent defeat of Austria in 1809 left little choice for these countries other than to submit to Napoleon. According to a treaty signed on 24 February 1812, Prussia agreed to allow French and allied forces free passage through its territory and to supply 20,000 troops for the invasion of Russia; Prussia would also provide the French military with necessary supplies. France likewise negotiated an alliance with Austria, which, having suffered four defeats at Napoleon's hands in the preceding 15 years, was in no position to defy France. Instead, Austria pursued a more conciliatory yet pragmatic policy, seeking to maintain good relations with France while Napoleon was on top of his game. In the new Treaty of Paris (14 March 1812), France and Austria pledged mutual support and Austria agreed to raise a 30,000-strong auxiliary corps that would report to Napoleon's supreme command in case of war against Russia. The ink was barely dry on the parchment when the Austrian diplomats assured the Russians that Austria would not pursue this war aggressively.

Although Napoleon's overall strategy for the war against Russia considered the use of Sweden and the Ottoman Empire to form his extreme flanks, he was unable to exercise influence over either power. Sweden – though led by a former French marshal Jean-Baptiste Bernadotte, now Swedish Crown prince Karl Johan – formed an alliance with Russia, which allowed Alexander to secure his northern territories and freed up Russian forces deployed in Finland. As for the Ottomans, their traditional alliance with France made them a natural ally for Napoleon, but their six-year war against Russia had been a failure, with their armies defeated and finances exhausted. In May 1812, Russia gained a crucial break when the Ottomans accepted the Treaty of Bucharest, which secured Russia's southern regions and allowed the Army of the Danube, some 60,000 strong, to move up and confront Napoleon. Moreover, as the war with France was underway, Russia celebrated two more diplomatic successes. On 18 July 1812, the Treaty of Orebro ended the state of war between Britain and Russia and pledged their mutual support against France. Two days later, in the Treaty of Velikiye Luki, Russia officially recognized the representatives of the Spanish *cortes*, which was waging a bloody guerrilla war against Napoleon; both sides pledged to coordinate their struggle against France.

Amidst his growing disagreements with the Russians, Napoleon launched preparations for war. New levies of conscripts were called from the 1811–12 classes, French garrisons in North Germany, particularly at Danzig and Hamburg, were reinforced, and the Grande Armée, as Napoleon's army came to be styled, assembled along Russia's western frontier. In late May, Napoleon set off from the Saxon capital Dresden to join his army. A month later, he was on the shores of the Niemen River, near Kovno (now Kaunas), reconnoitring the area and supervising the construction of large pontoon bridges across the river. The die was cast. The war, which Napoleon expected to be brief and decisive in his favour, would settle the differences between the two empires. And yet some of Napoleon's closest advisors did not share his optimism – Admiral Denis Decrès sullenly predicted at Dresden that 'Napoleon will not return from this war; if he returns, it will be without his army.'

Emperor Alexander was then attending a ball at General Bennigsen's country manor near Vilna, less than 60 miles south-east of Kovno, when, on June 24, his minister of police whispered in his ear that the war had commenced. He was not surprised by the news, for Russian intelligence had given him ample warning of the attack. Examining the military map, he could, however, see the immensity of the challenge confronting him. Russia had just 250,000 Russian soldiers to face up to the Napoleonic juggernaut. But even these troops were scattered among three major armies and a handful of separate corps that had been mobilized for the war. The First Western Army, commanded by General and Minister of War Mikhail Barclay de Tolly, held positions in the Lithuanian countryside surrounding Vilna. Further south was the Second Western Army, under Peter Bagration, whose units were spread out in the area between Volkovysk and Belostock (Białystok). General Alexander Tormasov

A portrait of Napoleon on horseback. (Author's collection)

The Russian First Western Army's commander General Mikhail Barclay de Tolly. (Author's collection)

commanded the Third Reserve Army of Observation that was gathered at Lutsk and covered the Ukrainian provinces. In addition to these three armies, Lieutenant-General Baron Faddei Steinheil's Finland Corps in the north and Admiral Chichagov's newly renamed Army of the Danube in the south covered the extreme flanks of the Russian army.

Alexander took the news of the French crossing of the Niemen in his stride, issuing a proclamation condemning Napoleon's aggression and urging his men to resist. 'We are left with no other choice but to turn to arms and appeal to the Almighty, the Witness and the Defender of the truth,' declared the Russian sovereign. 'The ancient blood of the valiant Slavs flows in your veins. Warriors! You must defend your Faith, your Country, and your Liberty!' Behind the defiant rhetoric, the reality, however, was grim. The Russian armies were no match for the assault that Napoleon unleashed against them. More worrisome than the inferiority in numbers was the nebulousness of Russian military strategy. Valuable time had been wasted in drafting and discussing various options – over 30, by one count – all of which considerably underestimated the enemy's strength and consequently were ineffectual. Ultimately, the czar lent a willing ear to Prussian General Karl Ludwig August Friedrich von Pfuel, whose strategy required the First Army to fall back to the Drissa fortified camp on the Western Dvina River while the Second Army turned the French flank and line of communications. Sound as the plan looked on paper, it ignored facts on the ground, for the Russians were outnumbered by at least 2:1. Barclay de Tolly and a small group of officers who surrounded him understood that neither of the Russian armies could stand and fight. They examined recent British operations in Spain and were struck by the Duke of Wellington's defensive campaign in Portugal, which had convinced them that the only way to prevail over Napoleon in Russia was through a similarly protracted and defensive war.

Retreat was the only sensible strategy and it soon produced results. One month into the war, Napoleon's initial plan to destroy Russia's armies in a decisive battle in the borderland had been frustrated. Despite their best efforts, the French and their allies had failed to catch their prey and were now hundreds of miles inland, suffering from attrition and diseases. The sheer size of the Grande Armée sapped its leadership's ability to cope with challenges. Napoleon raged about dilatory movements and the lax leadership of his subordinates; just eight days after starting the invasion, he complained that 'nothing gets done'. Internal reports and correspondence reveal the deep sense of uncertainty in which the French headquarters operated. Napoleon remained poorly informed of the enemy's positions and knew little of their intentions, the local terrain or routes; 'our maps are so deficient that they are practically unusable,' he complained just days into the invasion. Three weeks later, the Grande Armée was so far ahead of its supply trains that Napoleon was compelled to halt at Vitebsk to allow reinforcements and supplies to reach him. He mulled over his next steps and considered if it might be better to remain in the borderland instead of pursuing

General Peter Bagration, commander of the Russian Second Western Army. (Author's collection)

the elusive enemy further to the east. In the end, he decided to press on, convinced that the Russians would make a stand soon enough and that he still had plenty of time before the snow would come.

The Russian armies, meanwhile, faced a profound crisis. Their constant retreat had caused great consternation in the army and society; there were angry murmurs about the Russian military leadership and questions about military strategy. These grievances were exacerbated by an acute discord among the Russian aristocratic officers and the 'foreigners' who had gained influence at court and in the army. The latter had always been an important element of the Russian military, but Napoleon's victories in previous years had driven numerous foreign-born officers to Russia, with the German states furnishing the largest number of them. Their arrival naturally caused frictions with the native officers, who complained about the foreigners getting preferential treatment and usurping many senior posts in the headquarters. 'One hears nothing but German spoken at our headquarters,' complained one Russian official. Barclay de Tolly, the nominal commander-in-chief, was surrounded by a group of officers (many of German extraction) who supported his defensive plans. Opposing them was the much larger 'Russian party', led by General Peter Bagration (ironically, a Georgian), which urged an immediate counter-offensive. Anti-Barclay sentiments were so strong among the senior officers that they openly loathed the commander-in-chief and intrigued for the appointment of Bagration as supreme commander; some even called for Barclay to be removed by force. Bending under pressure, Barclay de Tolly agreed to a joint attack from Smolensk, but Russian-commander infighting and vacillation undermined this counter-offensive almost as soon as it started.

Napoleon's response was a masterfully conceived operation that transported over 150,000 men on a vast flanking manoeuvre that threatened to turn the enemy left wing and cut the Russians from Smolensk. Yet a resolute rearguard action at Krasnyi on 14 August enabled the Russians to delay the Grande Armée and prepare Smolensk for defence as their main armies rushed back to the city. On 15–17 August, the Russians repulsed French assaults on Smolensk but were nonetheless forced to abandon the city.

Moscow burns in September 1812, a painting by Christian Johann Oldendorp. (Fine Art Images/Heritage Images/Getty Images)

The surrender of Smolensk further aroused general discontent in Russian society. Emperor Alexander was pressured to act. In late August, he appointed General Mikhail Kutuzov as the supreme commander of the Russian forces. The 65-year-old new commander took charge of the Russian armies and withdrew them still further to the west before taking positions near the village of Borodino. Here, on September 7, in a savage and bloody struggle, both sides displayed incredible valour and claimed victory. The French, however, remained in possession of the battlefield while the Russian army withdrew in good order towards Moscow. A week later, in one of the most crucial decisions of the war, Kutuzov decided to abandon Moscow without a fight. In his words, Napoleon was like 'a stormy torrent' that was hard to contain by conventional means. Moscow, however, could turn into 'the sponge' that would absorb and reduce him to nothing. Entering the Russian capital, Napoleon would halt there since he would undoubtedly seek a political resolution to the conflict. This would be a mistake, Kutuzov knew, since the Russians had no intention to negotiate. Once inside Moscow, Napoleon would be absorbed, unable to squeeze himself out of the 'sponge'. The Russian army would meanwhile gain time to regroup, replenish and fight on.

On 14 September, Napoleon entered Moscow. Later that day, fires erupted and spread throughout the city and continued to burn until 18 September. The fiery devastation of the Russian capital city had a profound effect on the troops of the Grande Armée, as they were forced to billet amid the ruins, lacking proper provisions and shelter. Discipline became lax and many troops turned to pillaging. Kutuzov, meanwhile, skilfully redeployed the Russian army south-west of Moscow, where he established a fortified camp at Tarutino. Through this manoeuvre, the Russian commander covered the southern provinces, which were abundant with supplies and manufacturing enterprises. Kutuzov also began intensive preparations for future operations, receiving reinforcements that increased his army to 110,000–120,000 men, with additional forces to come. He remained determined to avoid a major

The Battle of Maloyaroslavets, 24 October 1812, by Nikolai Semyonovich Samokish. (Fine Art Images/Heritage Images/Getty Images)

battle and instead waged the '*malaya voina*' ('small war'), the main objective of which was to hinder movement of enemy reserves, interrupt supply deliveries, attack isolated enemy forces, conduct diversionary attacks, and, in general, reduce the effectiveness of enemy operations.

In mid-October, the Russian army felt ready for a counter-strike. On 18 October, Kutuzov attacked and defeated the French advance guard between the villages of Tarutino and Vinkovo. The Russian victory, incomplete as it was, marked a turning point in the war. It put an end to any hopes Napoleon may yet have cherished for a peace with the Russians, and made him rediscover 'the fire of his earlier years', as one of his generals observed. He instructed his marshals to start redeploying their forces from Moscow at once and to be prepared to leave at daybreak for a hard day's marching. Napoleon envisioned this movement as a strategic withdrawal, not a full-blown retreat, a point he repeatedly underscored. 'We are going to withdraw to the frontiers of Poland,' he confided to his trusted aide Jean Rapp. 'I shall take good winter quarters and see to it that Alexander will make peace.' The main route to Moscow had been utterly devastated when the French had fought their way in the summer, so Napoleon's best option was to move his forces through the south-western provinces of Russia, where supplies and magazines could allow him to sustain his army before resuming the war in the spring. Kutuzov, however, stood in his way. The Battle of Maloyaroslavets, fought on 24 October, was the third-largest battle of the war and had a profound impact on the course of events. Though a French tactical victory, the battle was a strategic defeat for Napoleon since it prevented him from reaching the rich southern provinces and instead compelled him to retrace his steps along the devastated route via Smolensk. The march to, and fight at, Maloyaroslavets consumed seven days – and this loss of time would prove fateful, as the Russian winter set in a couple of weeks later. The battle also signalled a change in the character of the campaign. Napoleon's strategic withdrawal from Moscow now turned into a retreat. From this point, the Grande Armée ceased offensive operations and sought to withdraw from the occupied provinces as fast as possible.

The Russians, on the other hand, assumed a more aggressive stance, which Russian/Soviet historians have traditionally interpreted as the start of the Russian 'counter-offensive', following Joseph Stalin's famous statement during World War II. But, in truth, Russian actions hardly constituted a counter-offensive. Despite significant numerical superiority, Kutuzov avoided open confrontation with Napoleon at Maloyaroslavets and insisted on the strategy of 'parallel march'. He envisioned Russian advance guard and flying detachments relentlessly harassing Napoleon along the central route while the main Russian army would maintain distance and proceed on a march parallel to the Grande Armée; if the opportunity arose, he intended to engage isolated French corps but otherwise remained wary of confronting Napoleon because the French would fight more fiercely to protect themselves (and their leader) and this would cost high casualties. Such a sacrifice, in Kutuzov's opinion, would be senseless when circumstances were so favourable to the Russians. His approach offered three key advantages: by shadowing the enemy, he could anticipate Napoleon's attempts to swerve into the fertile southern provinces, where the Russian army continued to draw its provisions; he could preserve the core of the Russian army and avoid losing men needlessly; and he could continue to harass the enemy through asymmetrical warfare. This strategy would play an important part in the events on the Berezina River.

CHRONOLOGY

1812

February–March Amid ongoing tensions with Russia, Napoleon signs treaties of military alliance with Austria and Prussia; both powers pledge to contribute troops to the impending campaign.

April In response to Napoleon's preparations, Russian Emperor Alexander I agrees to an alliance with Sweden.

May Russia and the Ottoman Empire sign the Treaty of Bucharest ending the six-year-long war. Some 60,000 Russian troops, serving in the Danubian Principalities, become available for the campaign against Napoleon.

23–24 June Napoleon's vast army begins to cross the Niemen River, initiating the campaign. The Russian armies retreat eastwards.

18–20 July Russia signs peace treaties with Britain and Spain.

19 July Emperor Alexander leaves the Russian field headquarters; Mikhail Barclay de Tolly assumes overall command of the Russian armies.

July Russian armies continue retreating. Russian victories at Mir and Romanovo are countered by French successes at Ostrovno and Mohilev. The French take Vilna, Minsk and Vitebsk.

4 August Barclay de Tolly and Bagration unite their armies at Smolensk.

8–12 August Russian armies launch a counter-offensive; Cossack Ataman Matvei Platov surprises a French light cavalry brigade at Moletovo Boloto/Inkovo.

13–14 August Napoleon crosses the Dnieper in an attempt to turn the Russian left and force the Russian armies to fight.

15–17 August The Battle of Smolensk. Napoleon is unable to gain a decisive victory as the Russian armies abandon the city and retreat eastward.

17–18 August Oudinot and Gouvion Saint-Cyr check Wittgenstein at Polotsk.

19 August The Russian armies check Napoleon's pursuit at Valutina Gora and Lubino.

20 August General Mikhail Kutuzov appointed as supreme commander of Russian forces and takes charge of the armies on 31 August.

7 September The Battle of Borodino. Kutuzov is forced to leave the battlefield but claims a victory in reports to the czar.

12 September The day after receiving Kutuzov's dispatch from Borodino, Emperor Alexander signs off on a plan that calls for three Russian armies, and as many separate corps, to converge behind Napoleon and cut off his escape routes.

14 September Napoleon enters Moscow, which the Russians evacuate; the city begins to burn that evening.

27 September Victor-Perrin's IX Corps arrives at Smolensk, providing much-needed reinforcements to the weakened main French army.

September–October	Kutuzov reorganizes and replenishes the Russian main army at the Tarutino Camp.
18 October	Russian victory at Tarutino/ Vinkovo; Napoleon decides to depart from Moscow.
18–20 October	Wittgenstein's victory over Gouvion Saint-Cyr at Polotsk exposes the vulnerability of Napoleon's left wing.
19 October	Napoleon leaves Moscow, intending to march through the southern Russian provinces that have not been affected by the war.
24 October	Kutuzov blocks the Grande Armée's southward manoeuvre at Maloyaroslavets. What started as Napoleon's strategic withdrawal now morphs into a retreat, as the Grande Armée ceases offensive operations and does its best to withdraw through the Russian provinces before it is too late.
3–4 November	First heavy snow; temperatures plunge to zero. The Grande Armée is experiencing an acute shortage of supplies, while lack of forage greatly weakens its horses.
9 November	Napoleon reaches Smolensk. After a four-day respite, he decides to resume the westward movement.
16 November	On its northward march, Admiral Pavel Chichagov's Third Western Army captures Minsk, with its vast supply depot.
15–18 November	Battle of Krasnyi.
21 November	Chichagov takes Borisov and secures the bridge over the Berezina.
23 November	Oudinot defeats Chichagov's advance guard at Loshnitsa and recaptures Borisov; the Russians destroy the bridge over the Berezina.
23–24 November	Wittgenstein fights actions at Chereya and Batura, pressing hard on Napoleon's wing.
26–28 November	Napoleon commences the crossing of the Berezina. Battles at Stary Borisov, Bryli, Stakhov and Studenka.
27 November	General Partouneaux's division surrenders at Stary Borisov.
29 November	With most of the Grande Armée across the river, the bridges over the Berezina are destroyed to hamper the Russian pursuit.
30 November	The French fight rearguard actions at Zembino and Pleschenitsy.
2–5 December	Rearguard actions at Dolginovo; Victor-Perrin's corps is defeated at Molodechno.
5 December	Napoleon leaves the army at Oshmyany.
8–9 December	Rearguard actions at Smorgon and Oshmyany.
9 December	The remnants of the Grande Armée reach Vilna.
10 December	The Russian army captures Vilna.
11–12 December	The survivors of the Grande Armée cross the Niemen at Kovno.
18 December	Napoleon reaches Paris and starts preparing for the spring campaign in Germany.

OPPOSING COMMANDERS

FRENCH AND ALLIED

With troops hailing from almost every corner of Europe, the Grande Armée's officer corps was ethnically diverse; but while officers at company level were mostly of different ethnic origins, general officers were largely French. At army level, out of 166 generals examined, 131 were French; and among 25 generals serving in the II and IX corps, which bore the brunt of the fighting at the Berezina, 21 were French, with the rest hailing from Holland, Portugal, Hesse-Darmstadt and Baden.

Of the 26 marshals Napoleon created during the empire, half participated in the Russian campaign. Two of Napoleon's most able marshals – Andre Masséna and Jean Lannes – were not present because the former was in semi-retirement in France, while the latter had died in 1809. Pierre François Augereau commanded a reserve corps in Prussia, while Jean-Baptiste Bernadotte had turned his back on his former comrades, having been elected Sweden's Crown prince. Four other marshals – Jean-Baptiste Jourdan, the hero of Flerus; Nicholas-Jean Soult of Austerlitz fame; Louis-Gabriel Suchet, the conqueror of Catalonia; and Auguste-Frédéric Marmont, Napoleon's close friend – were tied up fighting the British in Spain. Of the remaining marshals, 11 – Louis-Alexandre Berthier, Jean-Baptiste Bessières, Louis-Nicolas Davout, Laurent de Gouvion Saint-Cyr (who had just received the marshal's baton for his victory at Polotsk), François-Joseph Lefebvre, Étienne-Jacques-Joseph-Alexandre Macdonald, Édouard Mortier, Joachim Murat, Michel Ney, Nicolas-Charles Oudinot and Claude Victor-Perrin (known simply as Victor) – were with the Grande Armée in Russia. In addition, two future marshals, Emmanuel Grouchy and Józef Antoni Poniatowski, were present as well.

Nicolas-Charles Oudinot, Duke of Reggio. (Fine Art Images/Heritage Images/Getty Images)

Nicolas-Charles Oudinot (1767–1847)

'The Bayard of the French army', as Napoleon introduced him to Emperor Alexander, Nicholas-Charles Oudinot was a veteran of the Revolutionary Wars. His career, in many ways, exemplifies the new opportunities that the Revolution had created for ambitious and talented young men. The son of a brewer, he welcomed the revolutionary changes that opened the pathway for his rise through the ranks. Chief of Staff to Masséna in 1799, he helped plan the French triumph at Zurich and then commanded, to a great acclaim, his famed grenadiers across the battlefields of Europe. At Friedland, he held his ground for hours against a superior Russian army until Napoleon arrived with reinforcements to win the battle. He was an experienced commander who had distinguished himself as much by his tactical prowess as through his valour and resolve. His wife described him as 'kind-hearted, affectionate, and sensible', but also spoke of his 'iron will' that gave him 'the invaluable quality of endurance and tenacity'. The safest place on any battlefield, it seemed, was standing behind Oudinot, for he had been wounded over two dozen times, more than almost anyone else in the French army. At Friedland, a bullet went through both his cheeks, breaking two molars. 'These Russian dentists cannot even pull-out teeth well,' was his remark as his wound was dressed. Napoleon had a high opinion of Oudinot, and in 1809 promoted him to Marshal of France. Between 1810 and 1812, Oudinot administered the government of the former Kingdom of Holland before he was ordered to lead the II Corps during the Russian campaign. He was wounded at Polotsk but returned to his command two months later, just in time participate in the crossing of the Berezina, where he was wounded once more. He continued to command troops in 1813–14 and, after Napoleon's abdication, rallied to the Bourbon government. His last active service was during the French invasion of Spain in 1823, when he commanded a corps and briefly served as the governor of Madrid. He retired after the July Revolution of 1830 and served as the governor of Les Invalides in Paris until his death in 1847.

Claude Victor-Perrin (1764–1841)

The future marshal of France was born into the family of a notary and enlisted in the artillery as a drummer-boy. The Revolution opened careers to talent, and Claude Victor-Perrin took full advantage of it. He distinguished himself at Toulon and earned the rank of general of brigade in 1793. Sent to the Army of Italy, he served under Napoleon's leadership during the famous Italian campaign, and earned accolades for his leadership at Rivoli in January 1797. After commanding troops in the Vendée, he returned to Italy, where he was wounded at Trebbia in 1799 and performed well at Marengo a year later. Napoleon appreciated his talents and gave him high posts in Holland between 1800 and 1804, before dispatching him with a diplomatic mission to Denmark. In 1806, he served under Marshal Jean Lannes at Saalfeld and Jena, where the Prussian army was routed. In January 1807, he took command of the I Corps and performed admirably at Friedland, demonstrating a quick tactical eye. Napoleon made him a Marshal of France. After serving as the governor of Berlin, Victor went to Spain, where he scored victories over the Spanish army at Espinosa and Medellín before being defeated by the British at Talavera and Barrosa. Recalled to France, he assumed command of the IX Corps for the invasion of Russia, where he earned particular distinction covering the Grande Armée during the crossing of the Berezina. Surviving the retreat from Russia, Victor commanded corps at Dresden and Leipzig in 1813, but was subjected to Napoleon's violent reprimand for his dilatory behaviour at Montereau-sur-Yonne, which deeply hurt his pride. A grievous injury at Craonne ended his active service. He refused to support Napoleon in 1815 and remained loyal to the Bourbon

Claude Victor-Perrin, Duke of Belluno, in a lithograph dated 1832. (Universal Images Group via Getty Images)

king, who rewarded him with the post of minister of war between 1821 and 1823. He retired after the July Revolution of 1830.

A portrait of Louis Partouneaux. (Author's collection)

Louis Partouneaux (1770–1835)

A graduate of the Louis le Grand College, the 42-year-old Louis Partouneaux had been in military service since he began volunteering in 1791. Two years later, he fought and was wounded at Toulon (where Napoleon earned his fame) and later served in the Army of Italy. Praised as a capable officer, he was promoted to chief of brigade in 1795 and general of brigade four years later. In August 1799, he took part in the decisive Battle of Novi, where the Austro-Russian forces led by the famed Russian generalissimo Alexander Suvorov routed the French; Partouneaux was wounded and captured. After being released in late 1800, he was given commands in various military districts and earned promotion to general of division in the summer of 1803. He spent the next nine years in Italy, first leading a grenadier division and later commanding the French garrison in Naples. He was a brave, fastidious and efficient commander, but of an average talent, rarely rising above his peers. Still, one of the marshals characterized him as 'a distinguished officer who deserves benevolence from the Emperor; His Majesty does not have a subject more loyal and devoted to him'. Napoleon took notice. In March 1812, Partouneaux took command of the 12th Division of the IX Corps and participated in the invasion of Russia, which played a decisive role in his life. Left behind at Borisov, he was forced to surrender with his entire division; this earned him a sharp reprimand from Napoleon, who unfairly castigated him in the 29th Bulletin. The general spent the next few years living down the shame of surrender and trying to justify his actions at Borisov. Napoleon never employed him again, but the Bourbons did appreciate his talents and, in 1820, gave him command of the 1st Infantry Division of the Royal Guard. He died of apoplexy in 1835.

Józef Zajączek (1752–1826)

General Józef Zajączek. (Public Domain)

Nicknamed the 'Nestor of the Polish Army', Józef Zajączek had a long and diverse career. A scion of the Polish aristocracy, he served in the diplomatic missions to France and the Ottoman Empire, supported the Bar Confederacy, resisted the First Polish Partition, and spent several years in exile in France. Upon returning home, he became a member of the Sejm (Polish diet) and became an ardent supporter of the Constitution of 3 May 1791. He fought in the Second Polish Partition of 1792 and was a member of the supreme national council during the Kosciuszko Insurrection in 1794. Forced to go into exile, he joined the French army as a general of brigade in the Army of Italy in 1797 and commanded a corps of cavalry during Napoleon Bonaparte's Egyptian Campaign. Promoted to general of division in 1801, he took part in the Napoleonic Wars and helped organize a Polish legion in 1806. When Napoleon created the Duchy of Warsaw, Zajączek entered its service. In 1812, he commanded the 16th Division of the V Corps and was wounded at Smolensk. He made a full recovery and took command of the V Corps when Poniatowski was wounded during the retreat. Zajączek performed admirably at the Berezina, but suffered a grievous injury that claimed his leg. He was taken prisoner in Vilna and held in Russian captivity until the end of the war. From 1815, he became involved in the governance of the Russian-established Congress Kingdom of Poland, which many of his former comrades interpreted as treasonous behaviour.

General François Fournier-Sarlovese. (Author's collection)

François Fournier-Sarlovese (1773–1827)

One of the most dashing and colourful personalities in the Grande Armée, General Fournier was an archetypal hussar. The son of a petit bourgeois, he enlisted in the cavalry at the young age and, like many of his peers, supported the Revolution. With blue eyes, a thin moustache, a well-built upper body and a slim waist, Fournier cut a dashing figure of a cavalryman, but his character was full of contrasts. A women-charmer and a fine crooner, he was impetuous, and prone to violence and insubordination. His straight talking hampered his career, but he was excellent at Friedland, where his reward comprised a general's epaulettes. He later commanded dragoons in Portugal and Spain, where he became famous for his defence of Lugo. In 1812, he led the 31st Light Cavalry Brigade (in the IX Corps) with his customary panache and daring; his tomb proudly proclaims that he 'planted the Eagle on the ramparts of the Kremlin'.

Jean-Baptiste Eblé (1758–1812)

The name of Jean-Baptiste Eblé is forever connected with events on the Berezina and, as one scholar aptly put it, is to be uttered with all the 'honour and reverence' of a man who was 'in very truth a hero, upright, modest, self-sacrificing, and literally faithful unto death'. The son of an artillery sergeant, Eblé was 54 years old in 1812, having spent 39 of them in military service. After enlisting in the Auxonne Artillery Regiment in 1773, he spent almost a quarter of a century stuck in junior ranks before the Revolution opened up a career pathway. He became a general in 1793 and served with distinction in the Rhineland and Italy. Napoleon appreciated his talents, making him a baron of empire and the minister of war in Westphalia. In 1811, Eblé commanded artillery during the French invasion of Portugal and was present at the famous sieges of Almeida and Ciudad Rodrigo, before returning to Germany where Napoleon was assembling the Grande Armée for the invasion of Russia. Eblé commanded the pontonnier units and constructed bridges over the Nieman, Dvina and Dnieper rivers as the French made their way into Russia. During the retreat, Napoleon ordered the pontoon trains to be burned. Although he complied with the order, Eblé saved the key bridging equipment, and his foresight would play a decisive role on the Berezina. In later years, however, some French engineer officers complained that Eblé unfairly received the lion's share of the credit for saving the army.

General Jean-Baptiste Eblé. (API/Gamma-Rapho via Getty Images)

RUSSIAN

The success of the Russian plan to destroy Napoleon largely depended on the commanders entrusted with its execution and required a high level of coordination between them. Such coordination was hard to achieve, not only due to the vast distances

The Russian commander-in-chief Mikhail Kutuzov. (Author's collection)

involved but also because of the different and conflicting personalities of those who led the Russian armies.

Mikhail Kutuzov (1747–1813)

The Russian commander-in-chief was Mikhail Illarionovich Golenishchev-Kutuzov, a 65-year-old general who had spent most of his life in the military. Born into an ancient Russian noble family, he enrolled in a military school at the age of 12 and started his career three years later. He distinguished himself in the wars against the Poles and the Ottoman Turks, barely surviving two wounds to the head, and proved to be a talented diplomat who successfully carried out missions to the Ottoman Empire and Prussia. He was a capable administrator and military educator, and directed one of the principal Russian military schools, the famed Cadet Corps. Having fallen from favour with Emperor Alexander in 1802, he was called back to lead the Russian army against Napoleon in 1805. After the Austrian defeat at Ulm, Kutuzov's sound advice on avoiding battle and waging a war of attrition was ignored by Alexander, who called for an immediate offensive. The result was the calamity at Austerlitz, which was blamed on Kutuzov, and he spent the next four years in disgrace. In 1810, Kutuzov was given command of Russian forces in the Danubian principalities. Facing a familiar foe, he showed his military prowess by routing the main Ottoman army and negotiating a much-needed peace treaty with the sultan. These successes, together with his reputation for capable command, made Kutuzov a popular figure in Russian society, leading to his selection as the new commander-in-chief in late August 1812. He was a man of contrasts, inspiring and exasperating, of considerable personal charm and keen intellect, but calculating and artful. As a commander he was sometimes accused, particularly late in his military career, of being overly cautious, yet over his lifetime he displayed great personal courage on the battlefield. The scars on his face, along with 16 medals, including a complete set of the Order of St George for gallantry and military prowess – the first ever to achieve this – testified to his heroism and daring.

Pavel Chichagov (1767–1849)

Admiral Pavel Chichagov, commander of the Third Western Army. (Public Domain)

The commander of the Third Western Army was 45-year-old Admiral Pavel Vasilievich Chichagov. The son of an admiral, he graduated from the Naval Corps and began military service in 1779. Over the next decade, he distinguished himself fighting the Swedes in the Baltic, then resided in Britain for two years; upon returning home, he commanded various ships. The death of Empress Catherine II was a turning point in Chichagov's career. He was among the many officers who were dismissed in Emperor Paul's purges and spent two years in disgrace; the czar soon changed his mind, recalled him to active service, and promoted him to rear admiral, before changing his mind, imprisoning him, only to forgive and reinstate him once more. Chichagov's career prospects improved under Alexander, when he became a vice admiral and the minister of navy, and spearheaded reforms to modernize the Russian navy.

Contemporaries were deeply divided over this man, whose candour and honesty earned him many enemies. The admiral expressed his opinions bluntly, even when dealing with sovereigns.

Some found him 'a strange man' full of 'arrogance' and 'pretentiousness', but also praised his 'determination, firmness, strength of conviction and independence of spirit'. The relations between Chichagov and Kutuzov, never earnest, became strained in the spring of 1812 when Alexander dispatched the former to replace the latter as the commander of the Russian forces in the Danubian Principalities. The news of this appointment stunned contemporaries. 'What a strange idea it is to entrust a land force to an admiral,' quipped a visiting Swedish general. Kutuzov was not amused either. After months of hard campaigning, military victories and diplomatic negotiations with the sultan's diplomats, he was unceremoniously cast aside so an upstart admiral, lacking soldiering or diplomatic experience, could reap all the acclaim for ending the war. 'Sparing neither energy nor skills,' as he later put it, Kutuzov pushed the Turks to accept the peace treaty before the admiral arrived. They did, signing the papers just one day before Chichagov reached Bucharest. Both men thus felt slighted by these experiences: the admiral felt robbed of a chance to shape the peace and claim glory, while the general scorned the upstart who almost deprived him of his laurels. Just six months later, they found themselves tasked with intercepting Napoleon.

Peter Wittgenstein (1769–1843)

The 43-year-old Peter Ludwig Adolf Sayn-Wittgenstein-Berleburg was the son of a Prussian lieutenant-general and a Russian princess from the powerful Dolgoruky family. The young Wittgenstein was brought up in the family of his uncle, the famous Russian field marshal General Nikolai Saltykov, and started his career in the elite Semyonovskii Life Guards Regiment. He quickly advanced through the ranks, fighting the Poles, the Persians and the French. In 1805, he distinguished himself at Amstetten and Austerlitz. The following year, he briefly served against the Turks in Moldava before fighting the French in Poland, earning a golden sword for courage. Promoted to lieutenant-general in 1807, he earned the command of a corps, and in 1812 successfully commanded troops against the Grande Armée's left wing. After his crucial victory at Polotsk (18 October 1812) he was hailed (with some exaggeration) as the 'Saviour of St Petersburg' and was promoted to general of cavalry. A contemporary remarked that Wittgenstein belonged 'to those rare heroes who owe their fame not to fortune but to genuine military talent. Fearlessness, determination and personal courage were his essential merits'. But he was also characterized by vanity, arrogance and a lack of experience in commanding large units. He had previously commanded only at brigade level, and, his victory at Polotsk notwithstanding, his shortcomings as a military leader would be partly revealed at the Berezina, and fully the following year in Germany.

General Peter Wittgenstein. (Fine Art Images/Heritage Images/Getty Images)

Other generals and senior officers

These commanders were supported by a host of generals and senior officers who came from different backgrounds and experiences. On average, they were in their early 40s and had served in the military since childhood. Wittgenstein's and Chichagov's officers had honed their skills in two to four campaigns, most serving against Poland (1792–94), Turkey (1787–91 and 1806–12) and France (1805

Louis-Alexandre Andrault Langeron. (Fine Art Images/ Heritage Images/Getty Images)

and 1806–07), but some had also fought the Persians (1796) and Swedes (1808–09).

The 40-year-old Karl Osipovich Lambert was a French émigré officer who had fled his homeland during the Revolution and entered Russian service in 1793. He spent the next two decades fighting his former compatriots from the mountain slopes of the Swiss Alps to the frozen fields of Poland. In 1812, he distinguished himself at Kobryn and Gorodechnya and was promoted to lieutenant-general. Contemporaries thought Lambert was among the best cavalry generals of the era.

Louis-Alexandre Andrault Langeron was another French émigré officer, whom some compared to a 'soldier of fortune', while the Prussians described him as a 'miserable poltroon'; he returned the sentiment manifold. A veteran of the French expeditionary force during the American Revolutionary War, he fled France during the Revolution and entered Russian service. In 1805, he commanded a Russian column at Austerlitz, was unfairly blamed for the defeat, and sent to the Danubian Principalities, where he distinguished himself fighting the Turks. After 33 years of military service, Langeron had established himself as a competent general, but one who was also a constant faultfinder, incessantly criticizing his Russian comrades in arms. Still, contemporaries liked his cheerful character, for he was, in the words of a contemporary, 'constantly in a good mood, especially when fighting. With canister and bullets flying, a smile often graced his lips and he often made witty remarks'.

Ivan Vasilievich Sabaneyev played a crucial, albeit not necessarily affirmative, role in the events on the Berezina. 'One of the best officers in this army', as one British officer described him, Sabaneyev was 17 years old when he enlisted in the Russian army in 1787. By the time he stood on the shores of the Berezina, he was already a well-educated and experienced officer, having graduated from the University of Moscow and commanded Jäger regiments for over two decades. In 1799, while participating in Alexander Suvorov's famous campaign in the Swiss Alps, Sabaneyev was seriously injured and left behind along with other Russian wounded. He spent over a year in French captivity, but used this opportunity to get acquainted with French light infantry tactics. He befriended French officers and accompanied them to their training camps, where he observed and took notes on their exercises. Returning home, Sabaneyev prepared a special memo on improving Russian skirmishing tactics, and gained a reputation as an authority on this topic. He commanded light infantry regiments throughout the Napoleonic Wars, fighting the French, the Swedes and the Ottoman Turks. In 1812, he became the chief of staff of the Army of the Danube. Contemporaries spoke of Sabaneyev's literary knowledge, honesty and sense of commitment. In the words of Alexander Mikhailovskii-Danilevskii, Sabaneyev was a 'man of small and frail stature, shortsighted, wearing green glasses, mistrustful and quick tempered'. Contemporaries spoke of him as a man of contrasts – an intelligent, courageous and enterprising officer who possessed an abrasive character and, at times, was unable to contain his angry outbursts.

General Ivan Sabaneyev. (Public Domain)

OPPOSING FORCES

THE GRANDE ARMÉE

Despite having over a quarter of a million troops tied down in the Iberian Peninsula, Napoleon drew upon the resources of his vast empire to raise close to 600,000 men (not counting a veritable army of political officials, servants and attendant women) for a new war against Russia. Of these, just half were French; the rest were Poles, Italians, Swiss, Bavarians, Berg, Badenese, Württembergians, Hessians, Westphalians, Saxons, Croats, Mecklenburgians, Dutch, Danes, Spaniards and Portuguese, supported by two large contingents of Austrians and Prussians. The task of equipping, provisioning and moving such a multitude was colossal, requiring patience, money and organizational skill, which Napoleon amply possessed.

By June 1812, the Grande Armée had assembled along Russia's western frontier. Napoleon's main force gathered between Warsaw, Königsberg and Tilsit and consisted of the Imperial Guard, Marshal Louis-Nicolas Davout's I Corps, Marshal Nicolas-Charles Oudinot's II Corps, Marshal Michel Ney's III Corps and the three reserve cavalry corps under the overall command of Marshal Joachim Murat. The main army was supported by the Army of Italy of the Viceroy of Italy Eugène de Beauharnais, comprised of the IV Corps (Italians, Spaniards and Croats, led by Eugène) and General (soon to be Marshal) Laurent de Gouvion Saint-Cyr's VI Corps (mostly Bavarians). Further south was the Second Army, led by King Jérôme Bonaparte of Westphalia, which included General Józef Poniatowski's V Corps (made up of Polish troops) and General Dominique Vandamme's VIII Corps (Hessians and Westphalians), supported by Marie-Victor Latour-Maubourg's IV Cavalry Corps (Poles, Saxons and Westphalians) and General Jean Louis Reynier's VII Corps (Saxons). Marshal Jacques-Étienne Macdonald's X Corps (half Prussian) guarded the northern flank of the Grande Armée and had the task of advancing into Russia's Baltic provinces. The Austrian corps of Prince Karl Philip zu Schwarzenberg, supported by Franco-Saxon troops, covered the southern flank, and threatened the Volhynian provinces of Russia. Marshals Claude Victor-Perrin and Pierre Augereau, in charge of the IX (French, Poles, Berg and Badenese) and XI corps (French, German and Neapolitan units) respectively, formed the second and third reserve lines. Although the Grande Armée was divided into groups, the centre and right wing possessed little autonomy and remained closely controlled by the emperor, who, despite the enormous size of his forces and the vastness of the

Field Marshal Karl Philip, Prince of Schwarzenberg. The Austrian negotiated the marriage between Napoleon I and his second wife Maria Louisa of Austria in 1810. (Universal History Archive/Getty Images)

theatre of war (his forces were scattered over some 300 miles), stayed true to his principle of unity of command.

One month into the war, Napoleon's forces suffered considerable losses from combat, strategic consumption and desertion. The weather proved to be, as one French participant recalled, 'a veritable disaster for our troops', who suffered from heat and rain during those summer days. Owing to the state of the rain-soaked roads (which would have been poor even in good weather), the wagon trains laden with provisions and ammunition could not keep pace with the troops, who were constantly pushed forward by forced marches. Battles, supply problems and strategic consumption had reduced the strength of Napoleon's main force to fewer than 180,000 men at Smolensk in mid-August; a month later, when the Russians finally made a stand at Borodino, Napoleon mustered just 135,000 men. The ensuing battle was a genuine bloodbath that cost the Grande Armée some 35,000 casualties, including over four dozen generals.

During the month-long stay in Moscow (14 September to 19 October), Napoleon had moved Victor's IX Corps (over 35,000 men) to Smolensk and then directed it to support Gouvion Saint-Cyr's operations near Polotsk. He also took measures to rectify problems confronting his main force, which had increased in size to 115,000 men, but could not resolve the underlying issues of discipline and logistical challenges. When the Grande Armée left Moscow in late October, it was accompanied by thousands of non-combatants and an enormous baggage train laden with loot. Pierre-Armand Barrau, serving in the IV Corps, lamented the pitiful state of the army: 'Anyone who did not see the French army leave Moscow can only have a very weak impression of what the armies of Greece and Rome must have looked like when they marched back from Troy and Carthage.' The number of vehicles accompanying the army was truly staggering; traffic on this scale not only slowed the army's movements but also distracted the troops. French Colonel Charles Griois summed it up: 'This mass of men, horses, and vehicles resembled the migration of a people on the move rather than an organized army.'

The subsequent battles at Maloyaroslavets, Vyazma and Krasnyi, along with the cold weather that saw temperatures plunge below zero, had a disruptive impact on the Grande Armée and accelerated the demoralization

The Battle of Borodino, 26 August 1812, by Peter von Hess. (Fine Art Images/Heritage Images/Getty Images)

of its troops. At Vyazma, Russian Colonel Alexei Yermolov witnessed 'for the last time organized actions of the [French] forces that had previously spread horror with their victories and earned our respect. We could still see the skill of their generals, the obedience of their subordinates, and their energy. But there were no orderly enemy troops left; the experience and abilities of their generals were of no use now, discipline had disappeared, and soldiers seemed to have lost their last strength, each of them now a victim of hunger, exhaustion, and the cruelty of the weather'. The horses, having been poorly fed for weeks, were unable to resist the combined effects of cold, fatigue and hard-marching; they sank and stiffened by the hundreds. The enormous train of transports and artillery also began to diminish, as the roads were choked up with the spoils that had to be abandoned out of necessity as the means of transport failed.

French artillerymen hastily spike their guns and throw the barrels into the Dnieper at Smolensk. The illustration is by Faber du Faur. (Fine Art Images/ Heritage Images/Getty Images)

The four-day-long fighting at Krasnyi (15–18 November) was even more disastrous for the army, which had lost probably 10,000 men in action while the Russians claimed over 20,000 prisoners. The combat-ready core of the Grande Armée was now reduced to about 40,000 men with perhaps as few as 40 cannon; the cavalry branch was decimated – barely 1,600 men in the Guards cavalry, just a few hundred survivors from Latour-Maubourg's entire IV Reserve Cavalry Corps that had counted 8,000 sabres four months earlier. While the army still nominally counted 'corps' and 'divisions', these were all but skeleton units, many of the latter reduced to regimental strength. When Victor's troops encountered the retreating main army, or, to be precise, what was left of it, they were stunned to see (according to Philippe-Paul Ségur) 'a mob of tattered ghosts draped in women's cloaks, odd pieces of carpet, or greatcoats burned full of holes, their feet wrapped in all sorts of rags'. They stared in horror as 'those skeletons of soldiers went by, their gaunt, grey faces covered with disfiguring beards, without weapons, shameless, marching out of step, with lowered heads, eyes on the ground, in absolute silence, like a gang of convicts'. Colonel Griois lamented that the IV Corps comprised 'unfortunate men, broken by fatigue and stupefied by misery, who preserved enough energy for self-preservation alone'.

The leadership of the Grande Armée had undergone major changes during its four-month-long sojourn in Russia. The campaign would eventually claim nine allied generals of division and 21 generals of brigade killed or mortally wounded. At Borodino alone, Napoleon lost eight generals killed, among them two generals of division (Caulaincourt and Montbrun) and six generals of brigade (Compère, Huard, Damas, Lanabère, Marion and Plauzonne). On 18 October, generals Pierre-César Dery and Stanislas Fiszer were killed at Vinkovo (Tarutino). Alexis Delzons and Joseph Levie fell at Maloyaroslavets six days later; Czeslas Pakosz was mortally wounded at Minsk on 14 November, while Louis-François-Lanchantin fell at Krasnyi on 17 November. Besides generals, dozens of other senior officers – 53 colonels perished during this campaign – were killed, wounded or captured in the battles preceding the Berezina, thoroughly disrupting the command chain

The Second Battle of Krasnyi (or Krasnoi), November 1812, by Peter von Hess. (Fine Art Images/Heritage Images/ Getty Images)

that had made the Grande Armée such a fierce war machine in previous campaigns.

After events at Krasnyi, Napoleon made a serious attempt to rally the scanty relics of his once mighty force. The cold had, for the time being, lessened, and at Orsha there were magazines sufficient to make a sensible difference for the army. The disbanded soldiers were ordered, under threat of severe penalties, to rejoin their units. The various corps still retained their official existence but were shadows of their former selves. Davout's corps was reorganized into three battalions; Eugène's IV Corps and Poniatowski's V Corps included two battalions each; Ney's corps, after evading the Russian envelopment, was converted into three battalions; and Junot's VIII Corps had just a few hundred men left, effectively constituting a battalion. Of the hundreds of cannon Napoleon brought into Russia, only a fraction had survived until November, most having been lost to the Russians or spiked and sunk in lakes and rivers during the retreat. The surviving artillery, augmented by 36 guns found in Orsha and 30 cannon (from the Swiss regiments) detached from Victor, was organized into several batteries, which were then assigned to the corps. The surviving mounted cavalrymen formed the so-called Sacred Squadron in which, as Georges Chambray aptly put it, 'brigade generals were employed as lieutenants and colonels as sous-lieutenants'. How significant an effect these orders produced remains difficult to assess. Some sense of order did return to the corps, and units were refreshed and given food and ammunition from the magazines at Orsha, but the number of stragglers remained immense and it was impossible to compel the obedience of soldiers who were increasingly disheartened.

More effective were Napoleon's efforts to destroy superfluous vehicles that hampered the army's movement. He forbade officers and soldiers to possess carts or packhorses, and at one point even personally went to the bridge at Orsha where, as one eyewitness described, 'with a cane in hand' he performed the functions of wagon master-general for two hours. As transports entered the bridge, Napoleon asked drivers which unit it belonged to and made the decision to either let them through or had them abandoned. After Napoleon's departure, these measures were imperfectly fulfilled and few officers gave serious thought to enforcing orders; the mass of carriages and transports that crowded the bridges at the Berezina a week later testify to the degree to which the imperial commands had been followed. Napoleon's orders did produce, however, one crucial development that shaped the events at the Berezina. Among the transports selected for destruction were the surviving bridge train wagons, a portion of which had been destroyed in Moscow and then at Vyazma. General Eblé had managed to preserve a reserve train of 60 pontoons, but it employed dozens of horses that the rest of the army so desperately needed. Napoleon

French stragglers making a stand near Bobr in November 1812, by Faber du Faur. (Public Domain)

did not expect that Borisov would fall readily into Russian hands and was more concerned about the bridge equipages serving as a needless burden on the army. Sensible and necessary as Napoleon's intent to reduce the mass of transport was, his decision to destroy the bridge train was, in hindsight, the height of imprudence. In vain did Eblé implore to save a few pontoons – the bridge train was destroyed despite his protestations, and all he could save was two field forges, two wagons of charcoal, and six of implements. Demonstrating much-needed prudence, he had seen to it that each of his men carried tool, clamps and a fistful of nails. Such foresight would play a decisive role a week later, for without these implements the Berezina could never have been bridged.

'The Retreat from Russia' by Ary Scheffer. (Roger Viollet Collection/Getty Images)

The size of Napoleon's army at the Berezina has long been debated. No daily or weekly rosters were kept during the later stages of the retreat, and eyewitness testimonies vary greatly. Most sources suggest that the French emperor probably had about 30,000–35,000 men still capable of fighting, and as many stragglers and non-combatants trailing in their wake.

RUSSIAN

Russia confronted the French threat with military preparations that began in earnest as early as 1810. Reconnaissance missions had been dispatched to examine the area between the Niemen, Western Dvina, and Dnieper rivers, where existing fortifications were repaired and new fortresses, most notably at Bobruisk and Dünaburg, were constructed. In early 1812, the Russian command established a fortified camp near Drissa on the left bank of the Western Dvina River and a tête-de-pont fortification near Borisov on the right bank of the Berezina.

The Russian imperial forces tallied over 650,000 men but two-thirds of these were distributed throughout the empire. Some were situated in the Danubian Principalities, others in the Crimea, the Caucasus and Finland, leaving approximately 300,000 men with over 900 guns to face Napoleon's Grande Armée during the initial stages of the invasion. These troops were divided into three separate groups along the western frontiers of the Russian Empire. The First Western Army – 120,000 men with 590 cannon, commanded by General and Minister of War Mikhail Barclay de Tolly – held positions in the Lithuanian countryside surrounding Vilna, covering routes to St Petersburg and Moscow. Further south was the Second Western Army – 45,000 men with 168 cannon, under General Peter Bagration – whose units were spread out in the area between Volkovysk and Belostock (Białystok) protecting routes to Moscow and Minsk. General Alexander Tormasov commanded the Third Reserve Army of Observation (46,000 men, with 168 cannon) that was gathered at Lutsk and covered the Ukrainian provinces. In addition to these three armies, there was also a second line of defence consisting of Lieutenant-General Ivan Essen's corps at Riga; Lieutenant-General Egor Muller-Zakomelsky's I Reserve Corps at Toropetz; and Lieutenant-General Friedrich Oertel's II Reserve Corps at Mozyr'. The extreme flanks were covered by Lieutenant-General Faddei Steinheil's Finland Corps in the north and Admiral Pavel Chichagov's newly renamed Army of the Danube (44,000 men) in the south.

Once the military operations commenced in June 1812, the First and Second Western armies retreated to Smolensk, where they united but were unable to stem the advance of the Napoleonic juggernaut; bloody battles and arduous retreating caused such heavy casualties that only 111,323 men could be rallied in both armies in late August, when Kutuzov assumed the position of supreme commander of Russian forces. The carnage at Borodino claimed over 45,000 men, including 27 generals. A high proportion of senior officers were killed or wounded, which rendered some units inoperative; General Mikhail Vorontsov's Combined Grenadier Division had lost over 60 per cent of its 4,000 men. The Russian army was in no condition to give another major battle and needed a way to distract the enemy, to get him off its tail and gain the precious time to rest, replenish and reorganize.

After abandoning Moscow on 14 September, Kutuzov led the First and Second Western armies to the fortified camp at Tarutino, where he spent a month reorganizing it. In late September, he announced the merger of two armies into the Main Army (*Glavnaya Armiya*) whose strength increased from 75,000 to over 120,000 men, with an artillery train of more than 620 cannon amply provisioned and horsed. The number of available infantry leapt from 35,000 in late September to over 60,000 in mid-October; over two dozen Cossack regiments, each 500-men strong, had been raised, equipped, and delivered to Tarutino, raising the size of their force to over 15,000 men.

In late October and early November, the main Russian army engaged the retreating Grande Armée at Maloyaroslavets, Vyazma and Smolensk. Although its battle casualties were low, the strains of fighting a war in winter meant that, in just four weeks, the army lost more than one-third of its men from attrition, the elements, illness and lack of supplies. On 12 November, the III Corps mustered 8,286 men but had almost 6,000 men in hospitals; the 12th Division was reduced to 2,611 men after over 4,200 men fell sick.

A view of Moscow in 1807. The fire that raged in the city between14 and 18 September 1812 all but destroyed the city. (Chronicle/Alamy)

The Battle of Vyazma, 3 November 1812, by Peter Von Hess. (Album/Alamy)

The cavalry fared no better. 'Half of the troops in the army were sick,' commented a Russian artillery officer. 'In my company, less than a third of the men listed on the roster were actually healthy.' Ilya Radozhitskii, another artilleryman, reminisced about the dreadful conditions he experienced after departing the Tarutino camp. For days, he and his comrades could not find any shelter, as the wooden homes had all burned down and the few surviving ones were occupied by senior officers. Soldiers spent night after night in the snowy fields, barely warmed up by the meagre fires that illuminated the frozen ground. With their faces 'blackened' and their bodies 'wrapped in rags', some soldiers wore half-coats and others greatcoats. A few managed to lay their hands on special winter boots lined with fur; most could only dream of such luxuries. 'I myself barely survived that winter wearing a sheepskin coat and double felt boots while my head was wrapped in a large scarf,' remembered Radozhitskii. 'Enduring such hardship, we could not but marvel how the French, who were deprived of any means of subsistence and protection from the elements, managed to survive at all.'

After the victory at Krasnyi on 15–18 November, Kutuzov slowed down the pursuit. He sent forth the advance guard, along with various flying columns and Cossack detachments, but the bulk of his army proceeded forward so leisurely that it was soon entirely distanced from the Grande Armée. Kutuzov's lassitude has long been the subject of fierce debate, and contemporaries were far more vocal about it than the later generations of historians. Emperor Alexander wrote more than one harshly worded letter to the field marshal condemning his dilatory strategy, which, in his words, 'destroyed all the advantages'. State Secretary Vasily Marchenko confirmed the depth of the czar's exasperation when he noted that 'the ambiguity of Kutuzov's intentions and the steady stream of unfavourable news about him almost convinced the Emperor to recall Barclay de Tolly'. Kutuzov tried to reassure the czar that the situation was under control and that neither Wittgenstein nor Chichagov were facing immediate threat. 'The enemy army is no position to break away from me since I am constantly following on his heels,' he claimed. This was not entirely true, as the main army was not keeping up with the fleeing Grande Armée; in fact, in letters sent to his subordinates, Kutuzov discussed the possibility

An engraving by Edward Orme of the retreat of the Grande Armée from Russia. (Hirarchivum Press/Alamy)

of Napoleon rallying his forces and either attacking Wittgenstein or marching towards the Ukrainian plains.

Kutuzov knew of the hardship his men endured, and his decision not to press Napoleon too closely was shaped by two crucial and interconnected considerations. It reflected both his concern for the survival of the Russian army and the wider repercussions of Napoleon's defeat. Carl von Clausewitz, who was a staff officer in Russian pay, commented that Kutuzov saw his army 'melting in his grasp' and anticipated the great 'difficulty he would have in bringing any considerable portion of it to the frontier'. Senior Russian officers could see that the field marshal was reluctant to push his men hard because he was certain that 'the prolonged retreat, worsening winter weather, and raging hunger' would bring the French army to the verge of destruction without the involvement of the Main Army. He kept repeating, '*Tout cela se fondera sans moi*' ('It will all fall to pieces even without me') to those about him. With the outcome of the campaign all but determined, Kutuzov remained more concerned about the future. If Napoleon's military capacity was annihilated, what would happen to Europe? Would the fall of the French Empire unleash another period of political turmoil? What about the balance of power, and what would be Russia's place and role in it? These were questions with no easy solutions, but Kutuzov knew that in the harsh world of European politics providence favoured those with big battalions, so he was keen on ensuring that Russia had its share of them by not losing soldiers unnecessarily. Destroying Napoleon was not, in his opinion, necessarily in Russia's interests, for Britain would gain the most from the fall of its mighty continental rival. Napoleon's succession 'would not fall to Russia or any other continental power', the Russian supreme commander bluntly told a British commissioner who challenged his strategy. 'The succession would fall to the power that already commands the sea, and whose domination would then become intolerable.' Conversing with Prince Eugène of Württemberg, Kutuzov admitted that 'our young hot-heads are angry with me for restraining their frenzy. What they do not understand is that our current circumstances are far more effective than our weapons'. The war had been won and Russia stood to gain much from it; so, as Kutuzov put it, 'we cannot afford to reach the frontiers like haggard tramps'. Such an approach, however, meant that only Wittgenstein's corps and Chichagov's Third Western Army would confront Napoleon on the shores of the Berezina.

ORDERS OF BATTLE

GRANDE ARMÉE

Commander-in-Chief: Emperor Napoleon
Chief of Staff: Marshal Louis-Alexandre Berthier
By November 1812, the Grande Armée was in such a disorganized state that many regiments had just a few hundred men, and some had merged into temporary units. As a result, the precise organization of the army (below divisional level) is difficult to determine. The extent of disorder can be gleaned from Georges Chambray's estimate of the army's strength at Smolensk three weeks before the crossing of the Berezina:

Imperial Guard infantry	14,000
Imperial Guard cavalry	2,000
I Corps	10,000
III Corps	6,000
IV Corps	5,000
V Corps	800
VIII Corps	700
Dismounted cavalry	500
Survivors of the four Reserve Cavalry corps	1,900
Light cavalry attached to the corps	1,200
Artillery, engineer and gendarmerie troops	7,000

The II and IX Corps did not participate in the march to Moscow and back, and had therefore preserved their structure better than other corps.

II CORPS

Commander: Marshal Nicolas-Charles Oudinot, wounded; acting corps commander – Pierre-Hugues-Victoire Merle
6th Division (General Claude-Juste-Alexandre Legrand)
Brigade Albert: 26th Light Infantry Regiment (four battalions) and 19th Line Infantry Regiment (four battalions)
Brigade Moreau: 56th Line Infantry Regiment (four battalions), 128th Line Infantry Regiment (four battalions), 3rd Regiment Portuguese Legion (two battalions)
Artillery: 11th/5th Foot Artillery Regiment (eight cannon); 6th/5th Horse Artillery Regiment (six guns)
8th Division (General Nicolas-Joseph Maison)
Brigade Viviès: 11th Light Infantry Regiment (four battalions), 2nd Line Infantry Regiment (five battalions)
Brigade Pouget (Pouget was wounded, not present): 37th Line Infantry Regiment (four battalions), 124th (Dutch) Line Infantry Regiment (three battalions)
Artillery: 15th/5th Foot Artillery Regiment (eight guns); 1st/3rd Horse Artillery Regiment (six guns)
9th Division (General Pierre-Hugues-Victoire Merle; acting division commander – General François-Pierre-Joseph Amey)
Brigade Amey: 4th Swiss Regiment (three battalions), 3rd Croatian Regiment (remnants of two battalions mauled at Polotsk)
Brigade Candras: 1st Swiss Regiment (two battalions), 2nd Swiss Regiment (three battalions)
Brigade Coutard: 123rd Infantry Regiment (three battalions), 3rd Swiss Regiment (three battalions)
Artillery: 4th/7th Foot Artillery Regiment (eight guns); 5th/2nd Horse Artillery Regiment (six guns)
Corps Cavalry (General Bertrand-Pierre Castex)
5th Light Brigade (Castex): 23rd and 24th Light Cavalry regiments (Chasseurs à Cheval)
6th Light Brigade (Corbineau): 7th and 20th Light Cavalry regiments (Chasseurs à Cheval), 8th Light Cavalry Regiment (Chevau-Légers) (Polish)
Artillery and Auxiliary
21st/9th Foot Artillery Regiment (eight guns)
22nd/9th Foot Artillery Regiment (eight guns)
11th/1st Pontonnier Battalion
4th/3rd Sapper Battalion

III CORPS

Commander: Marshal Michel Ney
10th Division (General François Roch Ledru des Essarts)
1st Brigade (General Louis Thomas Gengoult)
24th Light Infantry Regiment (two battalions) (Colonel Julienne de Bellair)
1st Portuguese Line Infantry Regiment (one battalion) (Colonel Freire-Pégo)
2nd Brigade (General Louis François Lanchantin – captured at Krasnyi)
46th Line Infantry Regiment (two battalions) (Colonel Jean-Louis Brue)
3rd Brigade (General Jean-Baptiste Bruny)
72nd Line Infantry Regiment (two battalions) (Colonel M. Lafitte)
129th Line Infantry Regiment (two battalions) (Colonel Jean-Daniel Freytag)
11th Division (General Jean-Nicolas Razout – wounded at Krasnyi, replaced by General François d'Hénin)
Infantry Brigade (Colonel Pierre Pelleport)
18th Line Infantry Regiment (largely destroyed, fewer than 100 men)
4th Line Infantry Regiment (largely destroyed, *c.*80 men)
93rd Line Infantry Regiment (largely destroyed, *c.*100 men)
2nd Portuguese Line Infantry Regiment (largely destroyed, 25–30 men)
25th (Wurttemberg) Division (Major-General Ernst von Hügel and Colonel Schtockmeyer)
(largely destroyed, reduced to two battalions, fewer than 300 men)

V CORPS

Commander: Prince Józef Poniatowski – wounded, actual commander Józef Zajączek
(cavalry brigades detached to form a separate cavalry unit)
16th Division (General Józef Zajączek – wounded, replaced by General Franciszek Paszkowski)
Brigade (General Stanisław Mielżyński)
3rd Infantry Regiment (two battalions) (Colonel Ignacy Blumer)
15th Infantry Regiment (two battalions) (Major Maciej Rybiński)
Brigade (General Franciszek Paszkowski)
16th Infantry Regiment (two battalions) (Colonel Prince Konstanty Adam Czartoryski)
17th Division - General Jan Henryk Dąbrowski (wounded, replaced by K. Kniaziewicz)
Brigade (General Edward Żółtowski)
1st Infantry Regiment (two battalions) (Colonel Stefan Koszarski)
17th Infantry Regiment (two battalions) (Colonel Stefan Koszarski)
Brigade (General Czesław Pakosz)
6th Infantry Regiment (two battalions) (Colonel Jan Kanty Julian Sierawski)
14th Infantry Regiment (one battalion) (Colonel Euzebiusz Siemianowski – battalion commander Major Winnicki)
11th Artillery Company (eight guns) (Major Gugenmus)

5th Sapper Company (Captain S. Rakowiecki)
18th Division (General Karol Kniaziewicz – wounded, replaced by General Izydor Krasiński)
Brigade (General Stanisław Potocki)
2nd Infantry Regiment (two battalions) (Colonel Jan Krukowiecki)
8th Infantry Regiment (two battalions) (Colonel Kajetan Stuart)
12th Infantry Regiment (two battalions) (Colonel Maciej Wierzbiński)

IX CORPS

Commander: Marshal Claude Victor-Perrin
12th Division (General Louis Partouneaux)
Brigade Billard: 10th Light Infantry Regiment (one battalion), 29th Light Infantry Regiment (four battalions)
Brigade Camus: 125th (Dutch) Line Infantry Regiment (three battalions), Provisional Regiment formed from battalions of 36th, 51st and 55th Line Infantry Regiment
Brigade Blammont: 44th Line Infantry Regiment (two battalions), 126th (Dutch) Line Infantry Regiment (three battalions)
26th Division (General Herman Willem Daendels)
Brigade Damas: 1st Berg Regiment (two battalions), 2nd Berg Regiment (two battalions), 3rd Berg regiment (two battalions), 4th Berg Regiment (two battalions)
Brigade Hochberg: 1st Baden Regiment (two battalions), 3rd Baden Regiment (two battalions), Baden Light Infantry Battalion
Artillery
Badenese: four cannon of horse artillery; four cannon of field artillery
Berg: field artillery company and horse artillery company
28th Division (General Jean-Baptiste Girard)
Brigade Żółtowski: 4th Polish Regiment (two battalions), 7th Polish Regiment (two battalions), 9th Polish Regiment (two battalions)
Brigade de Villiers: Saxon Regiment von Low (two battalions), Saxon Regiment von Rechten (two battalions)
Artillery:
One company of Polish field artillery (six guns)
Corps Cavalry (General François Fournier-Sarlovèze)
Brigade Delatre: 2nd Berg Lancers Regiment (four squadrons), Saxon Regiment of Prinz Johann (four squadrons)
Brigade von Laroche-Starkenfels: Baden Hussar Regiment (four squadrons), Hesse-Darmstadt Light Cavalry (four squadrons)

VISTULA LEGION

Commander: General Michel Claparède (replaced by Colonel Stanisław Malczewski)
1st Vistula Regiment (Colonel Józef Chłopicki)
2nd Vistula Regiment (Colonel Stanisław Malczewski)
3rd Vistula Regiment (Colonel P. Fondzelski)

RUSSIAN

I SEPARATE CORPS

Commander: General Peter Wittgenstein
Chief of Staff: Major-General Fedor (Friedrich Auguste) D'Auvray
Quartermaster-General: Colonel Ivan Diebitsch
Chief of Staff of the Finland Corps: Major-General Alexander Fock
Quartermaster-General of the Finland Corps: Lieutenant-Colonel Alexander Teslev
Detachment (Major-General Yegor Vlastov)
Cavalry:
Finlyandskii Dragoon Regiment (three squadrons)
Loshilin's Cossack Regiment
Platov's 4th Cossack Regiment
Infantry:
23rd Jäger Regiment (one battalion)
24th Jäger Regiment (three battalions)
1st Combined Infantry Regiment: battalions from the Pskovskii, Moskovskii, Livabskii, and Sofiiskii regiments
2nd Combined Infantry Regiment: battalions from the Pernovskii, Rylskii, Ekaterinburgskii, and Selenginskii regiments
Artillery:
23rd Horse Artillery Company (eight guns)
28th Battery Company (six guns)
Advance Guard (Major-General Leo Yashvil)
Cavalry:
Gronenskii Hussar Regiment (eight squadrons)
Combined Hussar Regiment (four squadrons)
Combined Dragoon Regiment (three squadrons raised from replacement squadrons of the Pskovskii, Moskovskii, Kargopolskii, and Ingermanlandskii dragoons)
Rodionov's 2nd Cossack Regiment
Platov's Cossack Regiment
Infantry:
Mogilevskii Infantry Regiment (three battalions)
Podolskii Infantry Regiment (two battalions)
Navaginskii Infantry Regiment (two battalions)
2nd Jäger Regiment (two battalions)
3rd Jäger Regiment (two battalions)
23rd Jäger Regiment (one battalion)
25th Jäger Regiment (two battalions)
Three *druzhina* (squads) of the St Petersburg Militia
Artillery:
26th Light Company (12 guns)
14th Battery Company (six guns)
1st Horse Artillery Company (ten guns)
Right-Flank Corps (Lieutenant-General Faddei Steinheil)
1st Line: Lieutenant-General Ivan Sazonov
Mitavskii Dragoon Regiment (four squadrons)
Rizhskii Dragoon Regiment (four squadrons)
26th Jäger Regiment (two battalions)
Tenginskii Infantry Regiment (two battalions)
Tulskii Infantry Regiment (two battalions)
Estlyandskii Infantry Regiment (two battalions)
2nd Line: Major-General Vasilii Adadurov
Voronezhskii Infantry Regiment (three battalions)
Nevskii Infantry Regiment (two battalions)
Petrovskii Infantry Regiment (two battalions)
Litovskii Infantry Regiment (two battalions)
Three *druzhina* (squads) of the St Petersburg Militia
Artillery:
6th Battery Company (12 guns)
9th Light Company (12 guns)
28th Battery Company (four guns)
Left-Flank Corps (Lieutenant-General Gregor von Berg)
1st Line: Privy Councillor Alexander Bibikov
Permskii Infantry Regiment (two battalions)
Sevskii Infantry Regiment (two battalions)
Kaluzhskii Infantry Regiment (two battalions)
Three *druzhina* (squads) of the St Petersburg Militia
2nd Line: Major-General Ivan Kulnev
Azovskii Infantry Regiment (two battalions)
Combined Jäger Regiment (battalions from the 11th, 18th and 36th Jägers)
Combined Guard Cavalry Regiment (three squadrons raised from replacement squadrons of the Life Guard Dragoon, Uhlan and Hussar regiments)
Yamburgskii Dragoon Regiment (four squadrons)
Artillery:
5th Battery Company (12 guns)
27th Light Company (12 guns)
Reserves (Major-General Alexander Fock)
Detachment of Major-General Vasily Rakhmanov

Combined Cuirassier Regiment (four replacement squadrons from the Life Guard Horse, Chevalier Guard, His Majesty's Cuirassier, Her Majesty's Cuirassier and Astrakhanskii Cuirassier regiments)
Nizovskii Infantry Regiment (two battalions)
1st Marine Regiment (three battalions)
Detachment of Major-General Alexander Sibirskii
Replacement Grenadier battalions (three battalions formed from troops of the Leib-Gvardeiskii, Count Arakcheyev's, St Peterburgskii, Tavricheskii, Ekaterinoslavskii and Pavlovskii regiments)
Combined Grenadier battalions of the 5th Division (two battalions)
Combined Grenadier battalions of the 14th Division (two battalions)
Four *druzhina* (squads) of the St Petersburg Militia
Artillery:
21st Battery Company (12 guns)
3rd Horse Artillery Company (12 guns)
14th Battery Company (six guns)
23rd Horse Artillery Company (four guns)
Pioneer Company
9th and 15th companies of the 1st and 2nd Pontonnier battalions

THIRD WESTERN ARMY

(Excluding Lieutenant-General Osten-Sacken's corps [operating in the Brest region] and Oertel's corps [not involved in the fighting at the Berezina].)
Commander-in-Chief: Admiral Pavel Chichagov
Chief of Staff: Lieutenant-General Ivan Sabaneyev
Quartermaster-General: Major-General Burghardt von Berg II
Duty General: Major-General Alexander Ansio
Chief of Artillery: Major-General V. Rezvoy
Forward Detachment (Major-General Yefim Czaplic)
28th Jäger Regiment (three battalions)
38th Jäger Regiment (two battalions)
Pavlogradskii Hussar Regiment (eight squadrons)
Tverskii Dragoon Regiment (three squadrons)
Dyachkin's Cossack Regiment
1st Kalmyk Regiment
2nd Bashkir Regiment
13th Horse Artillery Company (ten guns)
Advance Guard (Lieutenant-General Charles de Lambert)
Infantry:
14th Jäger Regiment (three battalions)
38th Jäger Regiment (two battalions)
7th Jäger Regiment (three battalions)
Cavalry:
Tatarskii Uhlan Regiment (eight squadrons)
Aleksandriiskii Hussar Regiment (eight squadrons)
Starodubskii Dragoon Regiment (four squadrons)
Zhitomirskii Dragoon Regiment (four squadrons)
Arzamasskii Dragoon Regiment (four squadrons)
Grekov's 8th Cossack Regiment
Grekov's 11th Cossack Regiment
Melnikov's 5th Cossack Regiment
Barabanshikov's 9th Cossack Regiment
Evpatoriiskii Tatar Regiment
Artillery:
11th Horse Artillery Company (ten guns)
12th Horse Artillery Company (ten guns)
***Corps de Bataille* (Battlegroup) (General Louis-Alexandre Andrault de Langeron)**
(This *corps de bataille* also formally included the corps of Peter von Essen, left behind at Elizarov Stan for a special mission)
Lieutenant-General Alexander Voinov's Corps
18th Infantry Division (Major-General Aleksei Sherbatov I)
Vladimirskii Infantry Regiment (two battalions)
Tambovskii Infantry Regiment (three battalions)
Dneprovskii Infantry Regiment (three battalions)
Kostromskoi Infantry Regiment (two battalions)
9th Infantry Division (Major-General Ivan Inzov)
Nasheburgskii Infantry Regiment (two battalions)
Apsheronskii Infantry Regiment (three battalions)
Ryazhskii Infantry Regiment (two battalions)
Yakutskii Infantry Regiment (two battalions)
10th Jäger Regiment (three battalions)
Cavalry (Major-General Ivan Manteuffel)
St Petersburgskii Dragoon Regiment (five squadrons)
Liflyandskii Dragoon Regiment (five squadrons)
Severskii Dragoon Regiment (five squadrons)
Belorusskii Hussar Regiment (eight squadrons)
Kireyev's 2nd Cossack Regiment
3rd Ural Cossack Regiment
Artillery:
9th Battery Company (12 guns)
18th Battery Company (12 guns)
16th Light Company (12 guns)
17th Light Company (12 guns)
34th Light Company (12 guns)
35th Light Company (12 guns)
Kanatchikov's Pioneer Company
Reserve Corps (Lieutenant-General Ivan Sabaneyev)
15th Infantry Division (Major-General Fedor Nazimov)
Kolyvanovskii Infantry Regiment (two battalions)
Kurinskii Infantry Regiment (three battalions)
Vitebskii Infantry Regiment (three battalions)
Kozlovskii Infantry Regiment (two battalions)
12th Jäger Regiment (three battalions)
13th Jäger Regiment (three battalions)
27th Jäger Regiment (three battalions)
Cavalry (Major-General Peter von Pahlen)
Oliviopolskii Hussar Regiment (eight squadrons)
Derptskii Dragoon Regiment (five squadrons)
Kinburgskii Dragoon Regiment (five squadrons)
Saratovskii Infantry Regiment (two battalions)
Lukovkin's 2nd Cossack Regiment
Panteleyev II's Cossack Regiment
Melnikov's 3rd Cossack Regiment
Artillery:
34th Battery Company (12 guns)
38th Battery Company (12 guns)
39th Battery Company (12 guns)
25th Light Company (12 guns)
50th Light Company (12 guns)
16th Horse Artillery Company (ten guns)

The Russian plan to intercept Napoleon on the Berezina

OPPOSING PLANS

RUSSIAN STRATEGY

The strategic considerations underpinning Russian military planning had been circulating in the high command since the start of the war. The czar's advisors pointed out that by steadily advancing deep into the Russian heartlands, the Grande Armée was like an arrow whose shaft (line of communications) was all too easy to snap off. The czar agreed. On 12 September, the day after receiving Kutuzov's dispatch from Borodino, he signed off a plan that called for three Russian armies, and as many separate corps, to converge behind Napoleon and cut off his escape routes. Wittgenstein's separate corps, reinforced by the St Petersburg militia formed by Kutuzov and supported by Count Faddei Steinheil's Finland Corps, was supposed to seize Polotsk, drive Marshal Gouvion Saint-Cyr's forces back to the Nieman, and then threaten the Grande Armée from the north. Chichagov's Third Western Army – formed in September after the merger of the Army of the Danube and the Third Army of Observation – would secure the Belarusian provinces and attack Napoleon from the south. The operational goal, in the words of the czar, was to drive 'the Saxons into the Duchy of Warsaw, the Austrians into Galicia, the Prussians and Württembergers across the Nieman, while the French must be annihilated to the last'. While Napoleon waited in Moscow for a response to his peace overtures, Alexander envisioned concentrating over 100,000 men on the defensive line along the Berezina River, which would serve as an anvil on which Kutuzov's 'hammer' would shatter Napoleon's 'arrowhead'. If the plan were properly executed, the czar opined, 'not even the smallest part of the main enemy army would escape our borders'.

The proposed strategy had strengths and weaknesses. Napoleon's line of communication was indeed stretched over a vast territory between the Nieman and Moscow, and a setback on either flank would have dangerously exposed it. On

The evacuation of Moscow by the Russians in September 1812, by August Campe. (Fine Art Images/Heritage Images/Getty Images)

Cossacks pursue retreating French soldiers in 1812, by Auguste-Joseph Desarnod. (Fine Art Images/Heritage Images/Getty Images)

paper, the plan assigned sufficient forces to execute the double-pincer operation and correctly designated an area between the Dvina and Berezina as the bottleneck, a place where Napoleon's line of operation could be easily intercepted. However, the plan took little account of the mud, snow, cold and vast expanse of terrain that the Russian armies had to cross. Nor did it fully consider the fact that Napoleon still had considerable forces in the rear, with no fewer than five full corps present in the area where Wittgenstein and Chichagov were supposed to operate. More crucially, while effective communication and close coordination between the three Russian armies was an essential element of the plan, ensuring these lines of communication was virtually impossible considering the vast distances involved; failure to adhere to the agreed plan could allow Napoleon to engage and defeat each army separately.

Kutuzov received the 'St Petersburg Plan', as the czar's proposal became known, in late September, just as he was completing the Tarutino manoeuvre. He fully endorsed it (a point Soviet/Russian historians have tended to ignore) and communicated the plan to his subordinates, who began implementing it as Napoleon prepared to depart from Moscow. In October, having received Steinheil's reinforcements, Wittgenstein went on the offensive, outmanoeuvring and defeating Marshal Saint-Cyr's Franco-Bavarian forces at Polotsk (18–20 October) and shattering Napoleon's northern front line. Meanwhile, Chichagov left almost half of his forces to hold off the Austrians and Saxons in the south and marched the rest of the Third Western Army to Belarus. Just as the Grande Armée was being battered at Krasnyi, the admiral captured Minsk, with its vast supply depots, and Borisov, with its all-important bridge over the Berezina River.

The destruction of the Grande Armée on the marshy banks of this river would have been possible had the Russian commanders worked towards a common goal. But it was quickly apparent that such concord did not exist. Poor weather and vast distances made effective communications impossible, and the Russian commanders remained inadequately informed of developments in other theatres of war. Logistical challenges were compounded by mistakes, egotism and old rivalries. Chichagov allowed his army a longer rest at Brest-Litovsk than was justifiable by the necessity. The consequences of his decision were twofold: firstly, he missed an opportunity to drive back the Austrians and Reynier's VII Corps, and was compelled to leave a larger force under General Sacken to keep them at bay; and secondly, throughout the subsequent three weeks, the admiral was concerned that the Austrians might threaten his back. Equally at fault was Wittgenstein. In late November, with his corps just one march away from Borisov, he hesitated to move forward – the proud general, who had been lauded as the 'Saviour of St Petersburg' for his victory at Polotsk, had no interest in subordinating himself to the 'amphibious general', as some contemporaries derisively referred to Chichagov. Similarly, Lieutenant-General Friedrich Oertel, who was supposed to join Chichagov with 15,000 men of his II Reserve

Corps, found every possible excuse not to do so. His insubordination left Chichagov with about 30,000 men, a third of whom were cavalry, who could not fight in the swampy and wooded areas around Borisov. Chichagov was, understandably, furious. In a letter to the czar, he acidly noted that Oertel's misconduct testified to the fact that 'insubordination is often left unpunished' in Russia. 'Woe unto the armies that tolerate people like Oertel,' he concluded, before relieving the general of command and directing him to go to the Main Army to face a court martial.

What happened next offers a good example of the selfishness and division that plagued the Russian high command. Upon reaching the Russian headquarters, Oertel found powerful allies there who knew about Kutuzov's loathing of the admiral. Oertel himself seems to have been well aware of this and, according to Joseph de Maistre, disobeyed Chichagov to gain Kutuzov's approval. Certain senior officers at the main headquarters, Yermolov tells us, 'found a way to preclude Oertel from any responsibility for his insubordination'. Instead of being punished, Oertel was, in fact, welcomed at the headquarters and rewarded with the promotion to general-police-master of all Russian armies. It remains unclear whether Kutuzov was deliberately covering up Oertel's misdeeds or was misinformed by his savvy subordinates. His letters and reports suggest the latter. In mid-November, he was delighted to receive the admiral's dispatch informing him of the expected arrival at Minsk which, he thought, 'will have decisive consequences in present circumstances'. He then informed Wittgenstein that Chichagov would soon reach the Berezina with '45,000 men', which implies that the field marshal was under impression that the Third Western Army had been already reinforced by Oertel's corps and was, therefore, sufficiently strong to block Napoleon's advance long enough for Wittgenstein to strike from the north.

The relations between Kutuzov and Chichagov had long been strained, as they both remembered old insults and bore grudges. Their latest spat took place in May 1812 when Emperor Alexander sent Chichagov to replace Kutuzov as the commander-in-chief of the Russian forces in the Danubian Principalities, despite the latter's great victory over the Ottoman Turks. The Russian supreme commander had no love for the admiral, but the charges of him deliberately trying to sabotage the Russian military operations to deprive his rival of the credit for defeating Napoleon are misplaced. He did complain that Chichagov, despite having a sizable force, was acting 'somewhat unassertively' and was not 'reporting as to what he is doing'. The admiral responded in kind. George Carpenter, 3rd Earl of Tyrconnell, who served as an aide-de-camp to the British commissioner to the Russian army Robert Wilson but was attached to Chichagov, informed the British ambassador to Russia that 'Kutuzov's communications to the Admiral are not only infrequent, but extremely brief: he informs [Chichagov] about his location but provides no details on the enemy forces, his intentions, etc.'. Just a day later, Tyrconnell received private dispatches from Wilson describing the Main Army's movements, which he shared with Chichagov. The admiral was surprised by the details they contained and remained 'extremely dissatisfied' that Kutuzov's letters 'never contain

Lieutenant-General Friedrich Oertel's failure to join Chichagov with 15,000 men of his II Reserve Corps left Chichagov furious and resulted in a court martial. (Author's collection)

any significant information on enemy intentions, about which we are so keen to learn at the moment'.

Acting in a state of great uncertainty, the admiral compounded the problems with his share of mistakes. Instead of occupying the right bank of the Berezina, which offered a strong defensive position, he moved one part of his army to the left side of the river and set up his headquarters at Borisov. He did not identify local crossing sites and made no effort to protect the crucial wooden causeways, some half a mile long, that ran through the extensive Zembino marshlands on the western bank of the Berezina. Moreover, he failed to properly reconnoitre the area for enemy presence and ignored warnings that Napoleon might be closer than he suspected; a Russian officer found, among the half-burnt French papers, a dispatch stating that Napoleon would probably reach Borisov by 23 November. The news must have come as something of a shock to the admiral, since he remained poorly informed about the whereabouts of the enemy army. Yet he paid little heed to it, and his subsequent decisions were misguided. He pushed forward a small advance guard, allowed most of his baggage trains to cross to the undefended town, and permitted most of his cavalry to disperse to forage.

NAPOLEON'S STRATEGY

Reaching the town of Barany on 20 November, Napoleon weighed his options. He could select one of two major roads leading west: the Orsha–Borisov–Minsk direction, or the Vitebsk–Bocheikovo–Glubokoe road. The latter route seemed disadvantageous: it was poorly supplied and taking it would require Napoleon to march north, not west, losing precious time; more crucially Wittgenstein was threatening to intercept it. The Orsha–Borisov–Minsk direction offered better prospects, especially access to the vast Belarusian supply depots, but was not without its share of challenges. This road ran through thickly wooded terrain and, beyond Borisov, led to a narrow defile near Zembino. The greatest challenge was the presence of Admiral Chichagov's army. Napoleon had earlier received the news of its advance on Minsk, but according to his trusted aide Armand de Caulaincourt, 'the informant was unable to state exactly when [Chichagov] had started or how far he had progressed. All he knew was hearsay, picked up from someone else'. Napoleon anticipated that Chichagov would attempt to intercept him at the Berezina. 'As I have always thought, Kutuzov is leaving us alone now in order to head me off and attack me when [Chichagov] has joined him,' he told Caulaincourt. 'We must hurry to get to the Berezina, for that is where great things may happen.'

The morrow brought the devastating news of the Russian capture of Minsk (with its supply stores) and Borisov with its bridge. 'For the first time, the Emperor struck me as uneasy about the future,' noted Caulaincourt. And well he might have been, for he found himself in a very perilous situation. He had with him only 30,000 soldiers, accompanied by a helpless mob of thousands of stragglers, the majority of whom were in the last stages of misery and despair. The army had scarcely any cavalry left, its artillery branch was decimated. An unexpected thaw had melted the ice on the rivers, yet the pontoon equipment, so crucial to any river crossing, had been recently destroyed. With three Russian forces converging, the Grande

The Battle of Borisov, 21–23 November 1812

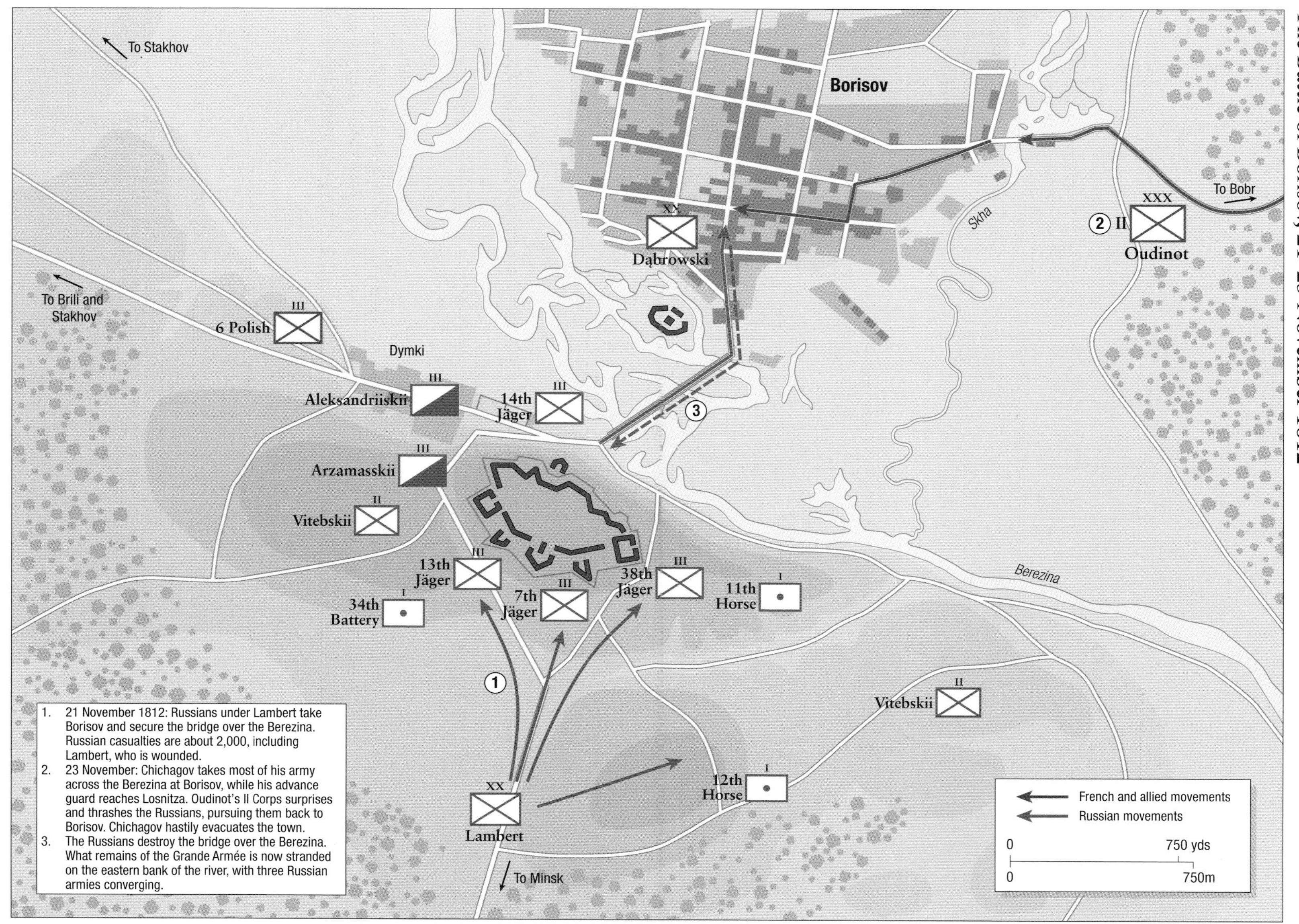

Armée would be outnumbered 3:1, and it seemed probable that Napoleon's whole empire might implode on the marshy banks of the obscure Belarusian river. This was the high point of the entire campaign for the Russians – the snare that the czar envisioned two months earlier was set and the emperor of the French seemed close to getting caught in it.

General Antoine-Henri Jomini, in a portrait dated 1811. Jomini, a Swiss officer, served as chief of staff of Napoleon's III Corps. He later entered Russian service. (The Print Collector/ Getty Images)

Napoleon sprang into action. He closely examined the area of operation and solicited input from his subordinates, including General Guillaume Dode de la Brunerie (in charge of II Corps' engineer troops) and General Antoine-Henri Jomini, chief of staff of the III Corps, both of whom were familiar with the area and knew its topography. Dode pointed out the difficulties of crossing the Berezina at Borisov while it was defended by the Russian army. The countryside was wooded, while wide stretches of swampland extended on both sides of the river; the wooden causeways that the army would have to traverse through this marshy ground could be destroyed, forming an insurmountable obstacle. The general suggested moving north to Lepel, where the Berezina was more shallow and easily fordable; reinforced by Oudinot and Victor, Napoleon could then brush aside Wittgenstein and clear the path to Vilna.

The emperor was not convinced. He objected to the proposal on the grounds of a lengthy detour from the main road and the possibility that the Russian armies could corner him between the Berezina and Ulla rivers. He favoured marching south, to Minsk, where he hoped to procure supplies and join Schwarzenberg and Reynier. Tracing the course of the Berezina and the Dnieper rivers on the map, Napoleon reminisced about Swedish King Charles XII's campaign in the area a century earlier. Spotting the small town of Poltava, the site of the great Russian victory over the Swedes in 1709, he quietly mumbled, 'Poltava, Poltava!' as his generals watched in silence. Other officers soon joined the conversation. Jomini's advice was particularly valuable – he had visited this area in August and September and had examined roads leading to Vilna. There were no favourable crossing sites south of Borisov, he explained, but the army would be able to cross the river just north of the town, where the river was more readily fordable; General Jean-Baptiste Corbineau, retreating with his light cavalry brigade, had already located (with the help of his Polish officers) a ford near the village of Studenka. Once across the river, Napoleon could proceed to Vilna by the road that ran through Zembino and Molodechno; if the Russians managed to block this route, he could make a detour to Vileika and still reach the Lithuanian capital. This suggestion was more to Napoleon's liking. Shortly after midnight on 23 November, he instructed Victor to guard the northern flank and keep Wittgenstein at bay, and ordered Oudinot to drive Chichagov's troops out of Borisov and secure the bridge; if this proved impossible, he was to secure the river crossing north of the town.

On 23 November, Oudinot struck at the unsuspecting Russian advance guard, thrashing and driving it helter-skelter down the road to Borisov. Chichagov, contentedly accommodated in the best house in the town, was about to dine with his officers when he saw Russian hussars galloping down the main street in mad panic and shouting '*Frantzouzi! Frantzouzi!*' The news spread like wildfire and caused pandemonium inside the town. 'Our people – cavalry, infantry, gunners with their cannon – rushed pell-mell towards the [Borisov] bridge, pursued by the French, who were charging with terrifying yells,' recalled General Langeron. 'One cannot describe the confusion and disorder that reigned at headquarters, which was imprudently placed close to the outposts.' Everyone fled headlong, 'abandoning their carriages and dainty lunches'. As his troops hastily re-crossed the river, the admiral, fearing that Napoleon would arrive at any moment, ordered the Borisov bridge to be destroyed.

This was a major setback for the Russians, who had lost more than 300 wagons filled with supplies, about 1,000 prisoners and six cannon. 'It seemed that Chichagov's officers took good care of themselves,' crowed one French officer, 'for never has such a profusion of hams, pâtés, smoked fish, meat, and wines of all kinds, not to mention biscuit, rice, cheese, etc., been seen in an army's supply train.' More crucially, the defeat at Borisov had shaken Chichagov's confidence and made him more circumspect about his next actions. He was also more hamstrung – driven to the right bank of the river, he could no longer effectively coordinate operations with Wittgenstein and Kutuzov, who remained on the opposite side. Defending the long stretch of the river was a daunting challenge, requiring close support from other Russian forces, and none was forthcoming. As the Grande Armée approached Borisov, Wittgenstein was miles away from the Berezina while Kutuzov, still near the Dnieper, had practically paused the pursuit. He sent forth the advance guard, along with various flying columns and Cossack detachments, but showed no intention to expedite the movement of the main army.

Napoleon, meanwhile, arrived at Loshnitsa, where he received the latest scout reports from the Berezina. The water in the river had risen significantly since Corbineau's fording and was full of large pieces of ice that could complicate the crossing; the frost that was setting in afresh was,

Napoleon gives orders during the retreat. (Bettmann via Getty Images)

Four of the marshals who accompanied Napoleon to Russia in 1812: Alexander Berthier, Édouard Mortier, Louis-Nicolas Davout and François-Joseph Lefebvre. (Author's collection)

however, beneficial, for without it not a carriage could get through the marshy banks. Another piece of good fortune was the presence of several villages that could serve as the sources of timber for the construction of the bridges. Napoleon also benefitted from the initiative shown by Marshal Oudinot, who understood the importance of distracting the enemy to ensure the army's passage across the river. Accordingly, he dispatched cavalrymen up and down the eastern riverbank, as well as a sizable force to the village of Ukholod', south of Borisov, to make a show of assembling timber and spread the rumours about the French planning to cross the river there.

This diversion has long been credited with deceiving Chichagov and compelling him to shift his army south. This is not entirely true and Oudinot's feint would not have worked if not for a perfect storm of mistakes, misjudgements and a failure of leadership. Russian reports and correspondence reveal the thick fog of war in which Chichagov operated. He was unaware of the depredations the Grande Armée had experienced since departing from Moscow and was still under the impression that Napoleon's effective strength was nearly 70,000 men, twice the size of the Third Western Army. Throughout those tense days, Chichagov worried that Napoleon might strike south of Borisov towards Bobruisk; this would have been strategically more advantageous for the French, for they could then recapture the vast supply stores at Minsk, draw sustenance from the fertile Ukrainian provinces, and receive succour from the Austrian corps. The admiral was not alone in dreading such a move; upon arriving at Wittgenstein's headquarters, Clausewitz discovered that 'every man was possessed with the idea that the enemy would take the direction to Bobruisk'.

Kutuzov, too, inadvertently came to Napoleon's help. In late November, he had written a series of letters that underscore the challenge of ensuring effective communications and intelligence gathering in a theatre of war that was several hundred miles wide. Upon hearing about Chichagov's entry into Minsk, Kutuzov warned Wittgenstein that Napoleon might be forced to leave the main road and veer northwards to reach Vilna. Anxious about such a possibility, Wittgenstein halted his march for three days. Not until 21 November did he venture to move his vanguard forward; if not for the delay in this advance, the Russian corps would have reached the Berezina in time to anticipate the French crossing and support Chichagov. Moreover, as days passed and Napoleon's northern attack did not materialize, Wittgenstein came to believe that the French emperor was in fact seeking an escape in the south. Consequently, he sent letters to Chichagov expressing his belief that the enemy must be moving partly to Bobruisk since Victor's IX Corps had been steadily falling back in front of Wittgenstein's corps; if Napoleon's goal was to reach Borisov, the general reasoned, Victor would have held his ground to protect the main road and the Grande Armée's right flank.

Meanwhile, Kutuzov made another inadvertent gift to Napoleon. Writing to the admiral, the field marshal instructed him to watch his southern flank. The letter did not command the admiral to redeploy his army, but the information, coming from the supreme commander, did carry weight with Chichagov; he was struck by the concordance of Kutuzov's and Wittgenstein's opinions and assumed these generals, who were better versed in military affairs than him, had good reasons for it. Napoleon's southern movement must have been true.

All Russian participants who served under Chichagov agree that Kutuzov's letter – which was based on the flawed intelligence supplied by his flying detachments – had a decisive influence on the admiral. 'I wish this dispatch had never reached us,' lamented Major-General Aleksei Sherbatov, for it convinced Chichagov of the need to move south. The admiral discounted reports of the French activities north of Borisov and assumed that Napoleon was more likely to cross the river downstream, probably at the village of Berezino, where there was a small bridge and a good road. Some of his senior officers disagreed. General Ivan Sabaneyev and Langeron tried to dissuade the admiral from making what they believed was a grave mistake, the former apparently losing his temper and getting into a heated argument with his superior. But none of it worked. Chichagov argued that he was not at liberty to simply disregard information provided by the supreme commander. He pointed to fresh reconnaissance reports that Austrian and Polish detachments had been seen probing the Minsk–Bobruisk environs; their goal, Chichagov argued, was to facilitate the Grande Armée's river crossing in the south so Napoleon could effect a junction with Schwarzenberg. Any lingering doubts the admiral might have had disappeared when French efforts to mislead the Russians through misinforming the local community – 'that wretched ruse', as one Russian officer commented – paid off, as local peasants rushed to the Russian camp with the news that the French were observed constructing bridge trestles near the village of Ukholod', south of Borisov.

On 25 November, much to the delight of the French, who were anxiously watching from the opposite riverbank, Chichagov led most of his army some 12 miles down the western bank of the Berezina, leaving just Langeron's division to protect Borisov and a number of loosely linked detachments (led by Major-General Czaplic) near Brili to observe the northern approaches. Yet the Russian misfortunes did not stop here. Observing the enemy troops massing near Studenka, Czaplic sent missives to Langeron and Chichagov warning them that Napoleon was intending a serious attempt to cross the river upstream. It took his messenger 24 hours to inform the admiral; in the meantime, Langeron, in a decision he soon came to regret, disregarded Czaplic's intelligence and threatened him with a court martial if he did not comply with the original order to fall back south at once. Receiving this harshly worded letter, the Russian advance guard commander had no choice but to comply. Czaplic ordered his vanguard to fall back and left behind only Major-General Kornilov's small detachment to observe the river and guard the crucial wooden causeway through the Zembino marshes.

THE CAMPAIGN

Just as Chichagov headed south, Napoleon himself reached Borisov, where he was observed by the Russian scouts – much to their consternation, as the only force at hand to oppose him was Langeron's small division. That day, the news arrived that Kutuzov's Main Army was still three days' march behind the Grande Armée. This report 'put the Emperor at his ease', remembered Caulaincourt. The situation was still critical, but Napoleon could breathe a little easier knowing that he had the advantage of time over the Russian commander-in-chief. According to Caulaincourt, he was confident that 'the issue was in his hands' and that he had enough time to get across the Berezina. 'Inform the generals that I intend forcing the passage of the Berezina tomorrow night,' Napoleon instructed his chief of staff. On his orders, generals Eblé (head of pontonniers) and François Chasseloup-Laubat (chief of engineers) travelled to the village of Studenka, about 10 miles north of Borisov, where they rallied some 400 pontonniers (2nd, 7th and 9th companies of the 1st Battalion and 2nd, 3rd, 4th and 5th companies of the 2nd Battalion) and as many sappers and the marines from the Danube Battalion to start constructing bridges across the river.

The Berezina, some 375 miles long, is one of the major rivers in Belarus. Rising in the marshes of the north-west, it flows south-east into the Dnieper, which carries its waters to the Black Sea. In 1812, the river was, on average, 20–30 yards wide upstream but, upon approaching Borisov, it widened and split into several streams that slowly meandered amidst the marshy banks that were prone to flooding in the spring and freezing solid in wintertime. The river was shallow and fordable in places, which probably explains why, even as late as 1838, it had only two major bridges, at Borisov and Bobruisk.

Present-day view on the Berezina River near Studenka. (Alain Poirot/Alamy)

Upon their arrival at Studenka, Eblé and Chasseloup examined the shoreline. Marcelin Marbot, the famed memoirist who served in the 23rd Light Cavalry (Chasseurs à Cheval), recalled that 'no enemy preparations for defence were to be seen on the farther bank, so that if the Emperor had kept the pontoons which he had burnt a few days before, the army might have crossed the Berezina on the spot'. Besides lacking the bridging equipment, the engineers faced another major problem: the recent thaw had melted the ice and increased the water level in the river, which was full of large blocks of ice; the boggy riverbanks were slushy and hard to pass through. Eblé and Chasseloup found 20 or so trestle frames already completed – General Claude-Aubry de la Boucharderie, Oudinot's chief of artillery, had been busy felling trees in the nearby woods and dismantling buildings in Studenka, a fair-sized village whose log cabins afforded timber useful for the construction of bridges. However, upon closer examination, the engineers determined that the trestles had been constructed of weak timber and were not solid enough to withstand the weight of the marching army. Eblé and Chasseloup had them dismantled and, with their engineers and their slender equipment, began in earnest to construct new supports for the bridges across the Berezina.

Old Russian log huts, like the ones seen here at the Mikhailovskoe Museum Preserve, supplied much of the timber for the bridges over the Berezina. (Maxim Mitsun/Alamy)

The original plan envisioned erecting three bridges across the river – two bridges would be built by the pontonniers and a third by the sappers and the marines – but it quickly become obvious that there were scarcely enough materials even for two. Marbot claimed that the river, which 'has been imaginatively described as of enormous width', was at most 'as wide as the Rue Royale in Paris, opposite the Ministry of Marine', meaning some 20 yards wide – but he most certainly meant one of the river shoulders. More knowledgeable eyewitnesses, including Antoine Chapelle, Jean-Baptiste Chapuis and Dutch Engineer Captain George Diederich Benthien who later produced detailed reports of the crossing, spoke of the river being hundreds of yards wide, with the half-frozen swamps extending a few dozen yards on either side and thus requiring the construction of longer bridges that would extend for some distance beyond the shorelines to facilitate the movement of cavalry and transports. Dozens of fascines had to be prepared and laid on the half-frozen marshes along the riverbank and small wooden rafts would be needed to install trestles in the deeper parts of the river.

All night the French and their allies laboured to prepare two dozen sets of trestles that were needed for each bridge. Lejeune remembered 'all the wood found in the village, even that of which the houses were built, being quickly converted into trestles, beams, planks, etc.'. François Pils, with his sketchbook in hand, recorded 'the preparatory work and construction of trestles was conducted behind a fold in the ground encasing the river and so preventing enemy scouts from seeing the workmen as they moved about'. Putting it all together with few tools and nails was an arduous job, but, at dawn on 26 November, the first supports were ready to be placed in the river; the engineers were employed in the preparation of trestles and floor planks while the pontonniers and sappers, many of them veterans of the Danube crossings of 1809, installed them in the river. Lieutenant Jan Chlopicki of the 8th Polish Light Horse (Chevau-légers) could see 'each trestle carried into the icy water by four sappers commanded by an officer standing on the bank and shouting orders, "*À droit!*", "*À gauche!*", or "*Lance!*" when its final position was confirmed'. There seems to have been an acute professional rivalry between the sappers, engineers and pontonniers, and at least one eyewitness described 'each

Construction of the trestles for the Berezina bridges as witnessed by Grenadier François Pils. (Author's collection)

of them claiming the sole right to build the bridges, with the result that they got in each other's way, and no progress had been made' (Marbot). In later years, some engineer officers complained that their contributions had been thanklessly forgotten while those of Eblé overstated; Colonel Paulin, who had, as captain, commanded the engineers of the 3rd Division of the II Corps at the Berezina, authored a lengthy pamphlet pointing out that the right bridge was in fact constructed under the direction of generals Dode (engineers) and Boucharderie (artillery) without Éblé's involvement.

Be that as it may, at this dramatic and decisive hour, the fate of the Grande Armée rested on the lean and tired shoulders of several hundred men who ventured into the frigid waters of the Berezina. Many of these men were French, but alongside them laboured Captain Benthien's 200 or so Dutch engineers and some 80 Poles from the 3rd Engineer Company (Captain Jean Fiedorowicz) and 5th Engineer Company (Captain Salvator Rakowiecki), assisted by Captain Jean Bujalski's 20 or so pontonniers. When called upon, these men stripped to their undergarments and, struggling against the river current and ice sheets, worked standing up to their shoulders in ice-cold water; Benthien described his men coming out of water stiff and half-dead. And yet the men answered the call of their chief with a heroism that some thought was 'superhuman' (Captain Rigau). Grenadier Pils watched as pontonniers 'went into the water up to their necks with a courage of which one can find no other example in history. Some fell dead and disappeared with the current, but the sight of such a terrible end did nothing to weaken the energy of their comrades'. And so the valiant effort continued. Oudinot's aide-de-camp (Le Tellier) remembered 'these men of duty and resolution marching silently into the water, never interrupting their work save to turn aside the huge pieces of ice which threatened to cut them in two like a sword'. The pontonniers drove in the piles and installed trestles, while the engineers laid down the planks. They kept on hammering until the moment came when they felt death seizing them, but others stepped in to complete their work,

The Berezina bridges by Victor Adam. (Public Domain)

Convergence of Russian forces on the Berezina, 15–20 November 1812

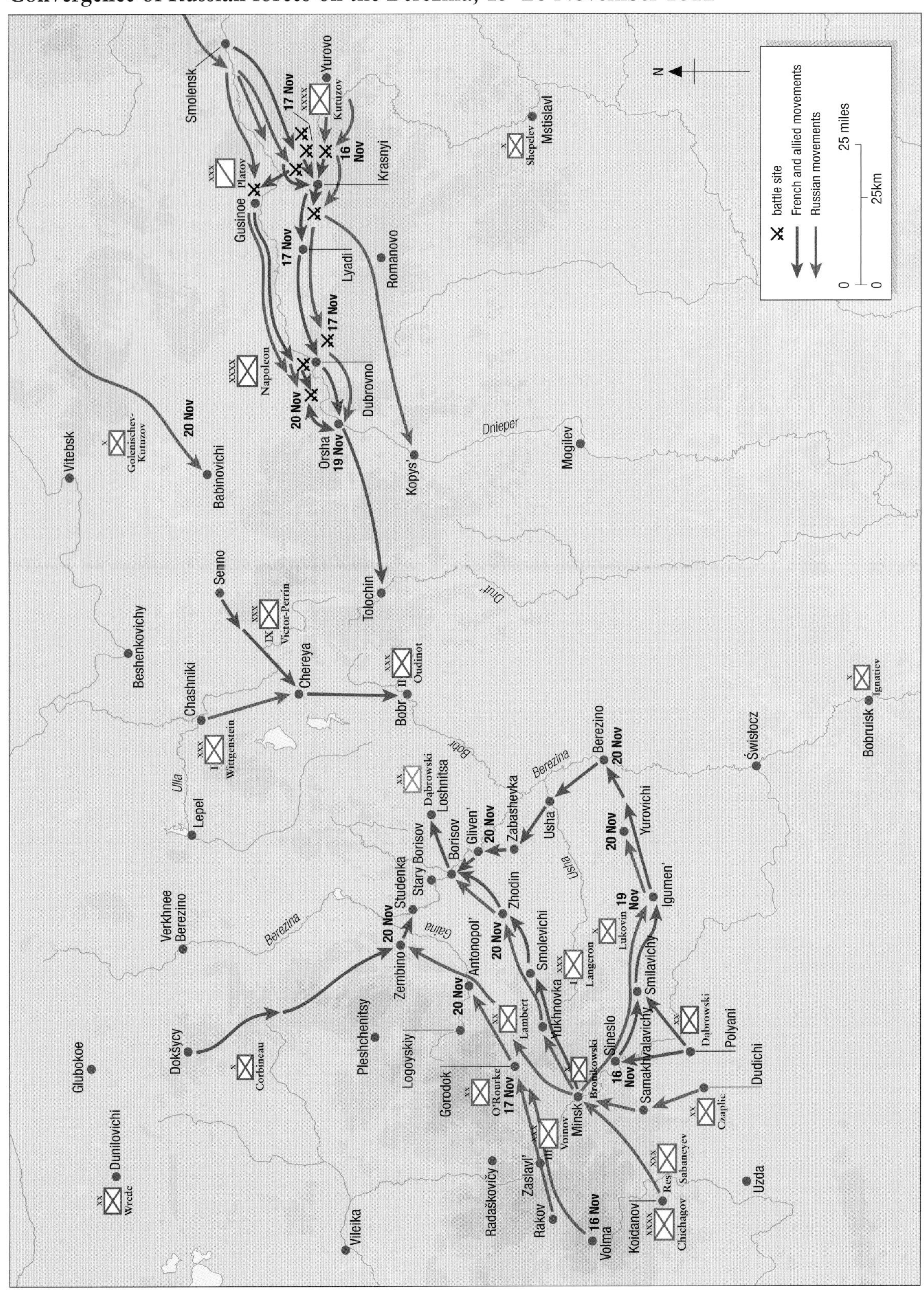

'the work of a day which should leave an immortal memory' (Le Tellier). The pontonniers were relieved every quarter of an hour but five-sixths of them perished; of some 200 Dutchmen Captain Benthien led into the waters on 26 November, only 40 were alive four days later.

This gallant sacrifice saved the army. By the end of the day, two bridges had been thrown across the river, each about 100 yards long and 200 yards apart. The left-hand bridge was intended for heavier transports, so most of the timber was committed to it to ensure that it was solid enough to withstand the weight of moving limbers, caissons and transports. As there was no time to square the planks that served as the floor, the bridge roadway was constructed of rough logs which caused the passing vehicles to jolt and shake the trestles, thereby impairing the stability of the entire structure; the pontonniers struggled to keep the supports steady and Bourgogne tells us that 'the trestles sank continually in the mud'. The bridge on the right was intended for troops, but it was constructed from timber leftovers from the other bridge and required almost constant patching; later that day, Maciej Rybinski, of the 15th Polish Line, saw a group of Polish and French pontonniers 'half immersed in the water', repairing the bridge. 'I told the officers in Polish, "These men are so devoted to their mission! This night they may repair the damage but tomorrow they will all succumb to cold and will die." They replied, "Yes, but the army will pass through."'

Looking at these hastily built bridges, Captain Heinrich von Brandt of the 2nd Regiment (Vistula Legion) justly remarked that 'from the point of view of aesthetics', they 'certainly lacked a great deal'. But when one considers under what conditions they were constructed and that for each life sacrificed in their construction a thousand lives were saved, then it became obvious that these bridges were 'the most sublime achievement of the war, perhaps of any war'.

DAY ONE: 26 NOVEMBER 1812

Napoleon, with his headquarters and the Guard, reached Studenka on 26 November. He examined the area and observed the bridge construction. Participants left contrasting accounts of how the emperor looked and what he did that day. Some described him in a fit of despair; Jakob Walter, a private in a Württemberg regiment, claimed that Napoleon's 'outward appearance seemed indifferent and unconcerned over the wretchedness of his soldiers; only ambition and lost honour may have made themselves felt in his heart; and, although the French and Allies shouted into his ears many oaths and curses about his own guilty person, he was still able to listen to them unmoved'. For Captain Louis Begos (of the 2nd Swiss), Napoleon was 'no longer the great Emperor I had seen at the Tuileries; he looked tired and worried'. Others saw it differently. Jean Calosso, of the 24th Chasseurs, could not recall 'a single sigh or murmur arising from our ranks' when Napoleon passed by. 'All our eyes were fixed on him ... we still had faith in his genius.' Other participants found the emperor energetic and keenly involved; he was seen helping with his own hands to serve out the precious alcohol to the fatigued troops. At one point, Westphalian Captain Johann von Borcke saw him standing near the bridge construction site and inspiring the troops with his presence. Jacob Anthony Tellegen, from the 128th Line, also observed the emperor 'at the bridge with Oudinot and at least 20 other generals behind him ... He was dressed in his grey coat over the Green Outfit, the outfit he cherished most.' Pils recalled the emperor watching the pontonniers 'without leaving the riverbank', while Berthier sat next to him on the snow writing out orders for the army. All sources agree that Napoleon demonstrated poise and confidence in what was a rather critical situation and did his best to rally and inspire his troops, even if occasionally betraying his own impatience while gazing upon the slowly progressing structures on which the army's last hopes rested. On at least one occasion he approached Eblé and urged him to expedite the work; the general simply pointed to the men working themselves to death in the icy river and the emperor could do nothing but walk away.

Napoleon observing the crossing at the Berezina, by Kossak Wojciech. (Artepics/Alamy)

The combat at Brili

Around 1pm, just as the right-hand bridge neared the opposite bank, Napoleon ordered Oudinot's corps, supported by Dąbrowski's Polish troops, to cross the river and secure a bridgehead on the western bank. The corps had suffered much in previous weeks but most of its regiments were still relatively strong and in good order; the Swiss and Polish regiments were especially in good order and eager. The first to cross the frigid waters was Colonel Jean-François Jacqueminot, Oudinot's aide-de-camp, with the survivors of the 7th and 8th Polish Light Cavalry (Chevau-légers), and the 18th Lithuanian Lancers, followed by several dozen riders of the 20th Chasseurs à Cheval, each of whom had a voltigeur (from the 11th Light) riding pillion. As the cavalrymen entered the river, the sharp-edged slabs of ice bloodied their horses but could not stop the brave men who swam to the other side, scaled the opposite bank, and engaged the Cossack outposts. Three rickety rafts ferried over infantrymen from Dąbrowski's Polish division, but as soon as the last planks were laid on the infantry bridges, the Swiss and Croatians of Merle's division and the French infantrymen of Legrand and Maison came across; one cannon and a howitzer (obusier) with caissons were carefully transported on the uneven, rickety bridge in their wake.

On the Russian side, Major-General Kornilov had only the 28th Jägers, two Cossack regiments and four cannon to confront the enemy attack. Captain Ivan Arnoldi, who commanded the artillery company, watched in exasperation as the French infantry spread through the woods and engaged the Russian outposts; the road was so narrow that he could set up only two guns in the clearing. He ordered his crews to fire at the bridge, but hardly had they fired their round when they were subjected to a formidable salvo from the 40 or so pieces that Napoleon set up on the escarpment across the river. Arnoldi had no choice but to fall back. It was a prudent decision, for Oudinot's attack unfolded rapidly, rolling back the meagre Russian detachment for a few miles before it was reinforced by Czaplic halfway between Brili and Stakhov. The II Corps had thus established itself in position before Brili, where it could cover the passage of the rest of the

THE NOBLE SACRIFICE: CONSTRUCTION OF THE BRIDGES ON THE BEREZINA, 26 NOVEMBER 1812 (PP. 48–49)

A recent thaw had melted the ice in the Berezina River; what would have been frozen and passable a few days previously was now flowing and full of large blocks of ice. When General Jean-Baptiste Eblé first arrived at the site, he inspected the trestles that had been constructed before his arrival and found most of them not solid enough to withstand the weight of a crossing army. He ordered new trestles constructed, with the homes of the neighbouring village providing a source of timber. Eblé decided to build three bridges: two were to be constructed by pontonniers, and one by sappers, assisted by the marines, many of them veterans of the Danube crossings of 1809. The night of 25/26 November was spent gathering material for new trestles and preparing planks and fascines. By early morning on the 26th, Eblé realized there was not enough material for three bridges and decided to continue work on two: one for the infantry and another for cavalry and transports.

In the scene shown here, it is late in the day of the 26th. In the foreground, a group of pontonniers are at work constructing one of the bridges across the Berezina. Trestles (**1**) have been erected in the freezing cold water, in which a few men are standing shoulder-deep as they fix the cross beams and secure the trestle tops. Other pontonniers are on rafts (**2**) assisting with this process. The pontonniers and sappers shown are a mixture of French (**3**), Dutch (**4**) and Swiss (**5**) and display a variety of uniforms.

General Eblé (**6**), in his engineer general's uniform and thick cloak, is atop the bridge directing the construction. A vast crowd of people, some soldiers, mostly stragglers, can be seen in the background (**7**). Also visible are the houses and farms (**8**) that are being dismantled to provide the timber for the bridges. Emperor Napoleon (**9**) is standing amid a small group of officers, observing the progress of the work.

Grande Armée; a small detachment of Polish chasseurs and lancers was sent to secure the passage to Zembino, where it surprised a Cossack outpost that was left behind with orders to set fire to the local bridges and wooden causeway that were already prepared for destruction. Had they fulfilled the order, commented the British commissioner to the Russian army, 'the route would have been irreparably closed against the enemy's progress'. Later that day, Polish staff officer Captain Ludwik Szczaniecki overheard Berthier telling Ney that the road to Vilna was free of the enemy. 'We have a completely free passage to proceed along. Victory is ours!' he declared.

Hearing the gunfire, Czaplic rushed to the front line and rallied his troops on the edge of the Stakhov woods. On the outskirts of Stakhov, Arnoldi finally found a position where he could deploy a 12-gun battery that, as he described it, 'began firing in every direction as rapidly as it could for the next three hours'. But as soon as he opened fire, his battery came under counter-fire from over three dozen French cannon that had been ranged on the rising ground behind Studenka and commanded the flat space beyond the river. The Jägers did their best to contain Oudinot's attacks long enough for further reinforcements to reach the battlefield from Borisov; Major Yakov Otroshenko, in charge of a battalion of the 14th Jägers, described 'a fierce fight during which we were driven into the woods. Both sides fought resolutely in this combat.' Russian sources describe the 38th Jägers, supported by the Tverskii and Kinburnskii dragoons, the Pavlogradskii Hussars and Cossacks, driving the French, Polish and Swiss troops back, though the fighting continued for a few more hours. Both sides suffered considerable losses and Oudinot admitted that his men lost 'a few killed but a considerable number of wounded', among whom was General Dąbrowski (lightly injured) and 'the intrepid' General Legrand, who was seriously wounded; the marshal asked Napoleon to replace the latter with General Albert, 'the most capable of the officers of his rank'. Delighted as he was to secure the bridgehead, Oudinot felt that more could have been done if he had been supported by Doumerc's cuirassiers, who had crossed the river late in the evening but played no role in the action at Brili. He complained to Berthier: 'If I had had cuirassiers, we would have achieved something outstanding today.'

As the fighting raged near Brili, the engineers and pontonniers completed the second bridge around 4pm. Minutes later, the artillery of the II Corps crossed over to the western bank, followed by that of the Guard. General Gabriel Neigre directed the passage of the 'grand artillery park' and hundreds of other transports. Caulaincourt, Napoleon's grand equerry, sent across the emperor's household transports and directed the drivers to go slowly and at some distance apart in order not to strain the bridge; the grenadiers and chasseurs of the Imperial Guard marched on either side of the vehicles.

As the news of the bridges being completed spread, Napoleon's valet Louis-Étienne Saint-Denis could see 'several generals, swords in hand, holding back the multitude who were pressing forward at the approaches to the bridge'. The sheer number of transports and people trying to cross over posed enormous logistical challenges. The movement of artillery limbers, heavy caissons, and transports had softened the swamps that had frozen overnight, turning them to a morass that impeded the movement of transports, the wheels of which sank deep into the mud. Furthermore, the hurriedly erected bridge framework could not withstand so much traffic, especially since, as Chapelle and Chapuis tell us, some drivers, eager to reach the perceived safety of the

General Jean-Baptiste Eblé rallying his troops, as sketched by eyewitness Grenadier François Pils. (Author's collection)

western bank, drove their carriages too quickly, bouncing and bumping on top of the bridge and causing some trestles to sink deeper into the mud, warping the bridge's framework. Around 8pm, the artillery bridge collapsed when three trestles subsided too deep into the muddy bed of the river.

The brave men who had spent much of the day building the bridge were warming themselves by bonfires when they were told to once again lower themselves into the frigid water in the darkness. Standing on the shore, Eblé directed their work, appealing to the engineers and pontonniers' sense of '*l'honneur et de la patrie*'. With the thermometer rapidly falling, the officers organized large bonfires and divided their companies into two groups, each working in the icy water for 15 minutes at a time. Baron Fain watched as 'braving the cold, fatigue, exhaustion, even death, they worked ceaselessly'. After three hours of agonizing labour, the bridge was repaired, and the movement resumed. Yet shortly after midnight, a few more trestles, in the deepest part of the river, collapsed. Once again, the pontonniers were called upon to wade out – some on rafts – into the ice-covered river, and, after several hours of work, they had fixed the bridge by dawn on 27 November.

Russian mismanagement continues

Chichagov, meanwhile, arrived at the village of Berezino only to discover that there was no trace of the enemy on the opposite bank. Earlier that day, he had received a new dispatch from Kutuzov who again directed the admiral's attention south and suggested that Napoleon, if unable to clear his way to Minsk via Borisov, would probably seek to cross the river at Igumen.

Retreat of the Grande Armée over the Berezina, by Franz Edler von Habermann. A section of the bridge has collapsed. (DeAgostini/ Getty Images)

Yet later in the day reports arrived that finally lifted the fog of war and revealed the full scope of the situation. First came the news that the enemy bridging efforts at Ukholod' were just a diversion. Then came increasingly desperate messages from Czaplic about 'immense enemy columns' moving north of Borisov and large enemy forces concentrating near Studenka. As the sun set that evening, Chichagov was aware of the fighting near Brili, but, as Major Yason Khrapovitskii put it, the admiral 'continued to hesitate, uncertain what was going on and whether the recent news was yet another diversion with which the enemy wanted to deflect his attention from the real crossing site' somewhere in the south. It was only after his scouts crossed the river and captured a Polish outpost at Pogost that Chichagov came to realize his mistake; rummaging through the captured Polish documents, the Russians found a letter that revealed Napoleon's intention to get across the Berezina north of Borisov. 'This evidence,' writes Major Khrapovitskii, 'had finally shown us that we had been misled and confused.'

Realizing the seriousness of the situation, Chichagov directed Langeron to 'hurry at once' with his division to Brili to reinforce Czaplic, while the rest of the Third Western Army, already worn out by a long march south over execrable roads, made an about-face and embarked on a forced march back to Borisov. The admiral also dispatched Major Khrapovitskii to Kutuzov with the latest news hoping the field marshal might expedite the movement of the Main Army and engage Napoleon from the rear. Alas, the major could not fulfil the mission on time – en route to the Main Army, he encountered General Adam Ozharovskii, commander of a flying detachment, who found the news so implausible that he had the officer held until he could confirm it. Kutuzov would thus hear about the events at Studenka and Brili only two days later.

Equally blameworthy was Wittgenstein's behaviour in the north. By 26 November, his corps had concentrated at Barany, just 20 miles from Borisov. Yet the Russian pursuit of Victor's retreating IX Corps was unenergetic and Wittgenstein, despite having double superiority of numbers, made no attempt to press on. Like Chichagov, he assumed that Napoleon had a sizable effective force and would try to cross the Berezina downstream from Borisov, his conviction reinforced by the reports of the French constructing a crossing near Ukholod' (a diversion, as we have seen). The Russian general thus decided to march to Borisov and did not change his mind even when confronted with the new information – a Russian scout reported that the locals had heard the sound of construction and gunfire coming from the direction of Studenka. General Ivan Diebitsch urged the corps commander to march towards the sound of gunfire at once. Yet Wittgenstein dismissed the idea, claiming the road would be impassable for his artillery. 'Let Chichagov deal with it,' he added. 'When the enemy leaves his tail on this side of the river, I will announce myself.'

This was a fateful decision. Had he marched directly on Studenka that afternoon, Wittgenstein would have played a decisive role in the battle on the Berezina and Napoleon would have undoubtedly suffered a heavy, maybe even crushing, defeat. But the 'Saviour of St Petersburg' chose otherwise. Clausewitz admitted that he could not understand the rationale for a decision that 'exhibited certain timidity and too great an anxiety for keeping the corps out of harm's way' and accused Wittgenstein of being directly culpable for 'the escape of Buonaparte'. He was not the only one. General Gregor von

Berg, who commanded the left flank corps under Wittgenstein, was also convinced that had the Russian forces marched to the crossing site, Napoleon would have had to either 'surrender to us or force his way through us'. But it was precisely this latter prospect that the Russian commander and his staff feared. The possibility of meeting the brilliant commander face to face in battle, without any hope of receiving support from the Main Army, clearly influenced their thinking. Wittgenstein preferred a safer option of leading the corps to Borisov on what Berg branded as 'that vile side march'. The senior Russian officers were very disappointed with this decision, which remained 'a great secret amongst us' (Berg) even as Chichagov was unfairly blamed for Napoleon's escape. What precisely happened that evening was never examined; the war had already been won by that point, and no one wanted to dredge up past misdeeds. 'Neither I nor any of those who knew the matter in our corps ever spoke of it so as not to harm our beloved count,' Berg admitted.

DAY TWO: 27 NOVEMBER 1812

The night of 26/27 November was cold but quiet. 'The calendar shows it is the Day of Repentance and Prayer today,' Otto Raven, a young officer from Mecklenburg, ruefully jotted down in his diary. Snow began to fall in thick flakes. On the western bank, Louis Begos and his comrades from the 2nd Swiss Regiment spent the night inside the snow-covered woods. 'An icy wind was blowing hard. To keep each other warm, our men lay closely huddled together,' he recalled. 'We had not eaten anything all day long.'

As the sun rose that morning, the remainder of the Grande Armée began to arrive at Studenka. Lieutenant Albrecht von Muraldt of the 4th Bavarian Light Cavalry (from Ornano's light cavalry brigade) saw the riverbank in front of the bridges 'covered as far as the eye could see with cannon, caissons and all kinds of vehicles, [and] a variegated mass was crowding together. Among this mass of troops of all ranks and arms one seldom saw anything reminiscent of a complete uniform'. The troops were famished, having had nothing to eat for the past few days. Westphalian Jakob Walter could find

A pitiful scene of the Grande Armée crossing the Berezina, as seen by Faber du Faur. (Public Domain)

The night bivouac of the Grande Armée, by Vasilii Vereschagin. (Public Domain)

nothing but some 'raw bran in which there was hardly a dust of flour', but which he mixed with snow to form 'a lump about the size of my fist' that he consumed 'with the heartiest appetite'.

'The ice floating down the river makes the bridges very unstable,' Napoleon complained in a letter to his foreign minister on 27 November. Indeed, the bridges suffered from recurring collapses that delayed the crossing, but the engineers and pontonniers made the necessary repairs and the movement continued. It was a grimy and chaotic experience. Mud and detritus covered the surface of both bridges and, as many surface planks cracked, horses broke their legs after falling through the gaps; the wretched creatures were then shot or thrown off the bridge so the endless column of transports could move forward. What was left of the Ney's III Corps crossed at dawn and was soon joined by the Polish divisions of the V Corps and the Guard artillery companies. A few hours later, the Vistula Legion crossed over too; the wounded Captain Heinrich von Brandt, of the 2nd Vistula Regiment, described units 'drawn up alongside one another in battalion columns' as they readied for the crossing. Around 1pm, the emperor himself crossed the river, followed by the rest of the Imperial Guard. Baron Fain watched as Marshal Lefebvre laboured tirelessly to get his men across: 'This old warrior, who had not shaved for several days, was adorned with a white beard and was leaning on a traveller's stick, which in his hands had become a noble marshal's baton.' In the afternoon, Eugène and Davout reached Studenka, bivouacking their men on the heights along the eastern bank. Labaume claims that many of his comrades from the IV Corps could not 'tear themselves away from the bonfires they had lighted, arguing that it was just as well to wait until next day, when the bridges would be clearer of people'. A portion of the IV Corps thus remained on the eastern bank while the rest crossed along with Davout's I Corps and the survivors of the once resplendent reserve cavalry corps.

By midnight on 27 November, Napoleon had thus moved most of his effective forces – I, II, III, IV and V corps plus the Imperial Guard – safely across the river. The crossing was an orderly affair regulated by the Elite Gendarmes, whose tidy uniforms contrasted with those of the worn-out masses that trudged across the bridges. Except for an occasional bridge collapse, there was no significant obstruction to the movement of troops and transports. It remains unclear how many of the non-combatants might have crossed that day but there should not have been too many of them. Actress Louise Fusil was one of the fortunate ones. Travelling in a marshal's carriage, she reached the crossing site on the 27th and was surprised to see Napoleon still at the bridge. 'To me he seemed as calm as at a review at the Tuileries. The bridge was so narrow that our carriage almost touched him. "Do not be afraid," he said, "Move on. Do not be afraid."'

The vast majority of stragglers was, then, at Borisov, where Colonel Griois witnessed 'unimaginable disorder'. He described thousands of stragglers, accompanied with numerous carriages and transports, jamming the streets. Victor's men had to fight their way through crowds in order to clear the path. People were shoving each other; curses and expletives could be heard all around. By nightfall, this multitude of famished, cold, sick and wearied men and women reached the crossing site at Studenka. 'Their disorganized march caused such confusion that it was only through immense hardship and great danger that one could reach the bridges,' lamented Chapelle and Chapuis. The gendarmes had to resort to force to hold back the surging throngs of people. Carriages, wagons and other transports, however, kept converging on the crossing site from all directions, blocking all approaches and inciting countless quarrels. Men were fighting for places and possessions; the strong trampled the weak. Polish Captain Józef Kozłowski (9th Infantry Regiment of the Grand Duchy of Warsaw) watched in bewilderment as the entrance to the infantry bridge became 'covered with corpses over which people strode to get onto the bridge'. The once valiant Grande Armée, wrote François Dumonceau (2nd Chevau-légers Lanciers of the Imperial Guard), had become 'an assembly of thousands of men of all arms, soldiers, officers, even generals, all mixed up, covered in the filthiest rags and grotesquely

The retreat of the Grande Armée, by Carl Röchling, (Public Domain)

A British print condemning Napoleon for 'barbarous and inhuman conduct' in abandoning the sick and the wounded. In reality, Napoleon did as much as he could to keep the bridges intact for the stragglers to cross over. Many of them, however, showed unusual complacence and stayed at the bivouacs. (The Picture Art Collection/Alamy)

disposed to protect themselves ... Their faces [were] downcast by exhaustion, pale, sinister, smoke-blackened, often mutilated by frostbite, the eyes hollow, extinct, hair in disorder, the beard long and disgusting'.

As the number of people seeking to cross the river increased, Napoleon instructed the gendarmes to tighten control of the movement, but enforcing any kind of order among the stragglers proved impossible. The crowd kept shoving and pushing to get across the bridges and the pontonniers and gendarmes at the bridgeheads were struggling violently with them to contain and regulate their passage. 'This only resulted in shouts, vociferations and terrible commotion,' observed Dumonceau. Still, even amidst this mayhem there were glimpses of humanity. Dominique Larrey, the Surgeon General of the Grande Armée whom everyone revered, was let through to the shouts of 'Let us save him who has saved us!'

Perhaps the most incredible feature of the crossing was an unusual complacence that descended on the eastern bank after the sun set. As the darkness shrouded the area and the frost intensified, many non-combatants became content and preferred to enjoy the warmth of bonfires rather than brave the crossing in darkness and cold. The bridges remained virtually empty and there was ample opportunity that long winter night to cross the river. Yet the fatigued and sleepy men and women paid little attention to calls to move on. Sergeant Bourgogne was startled to see 'everyone at their bivouacs and no one crossing over the [foot] bridge during the night, a most astonishing thing'. Their senses numbed by the utter misery of the retreat, the stragglers settled down by their fires and lost all sense of the urgency of their situation. Some collapsed from exhaustion, others tried to find morsels of food, and a few sought to exploit an opportunity to enrich themselves.

Napoleon's success in moving most of his army across the river owed much to the continued Russian slothfulness. Kutuzov and Wittgenstein 'abandoned me with my meagre forces to face Napoleon, his marshals and an army that was three times larger than mine', complained Chichagov, who was furious that neither commander was in position to support him – Kutuzov was still at least three days' march away from the Berezina, while Wittgenstein was slowly following Victor, never pressing him too closely. The admiral reached Borisov in the evening of the 27th but most of his

Situation on the Berezina, 22–25 November 1812

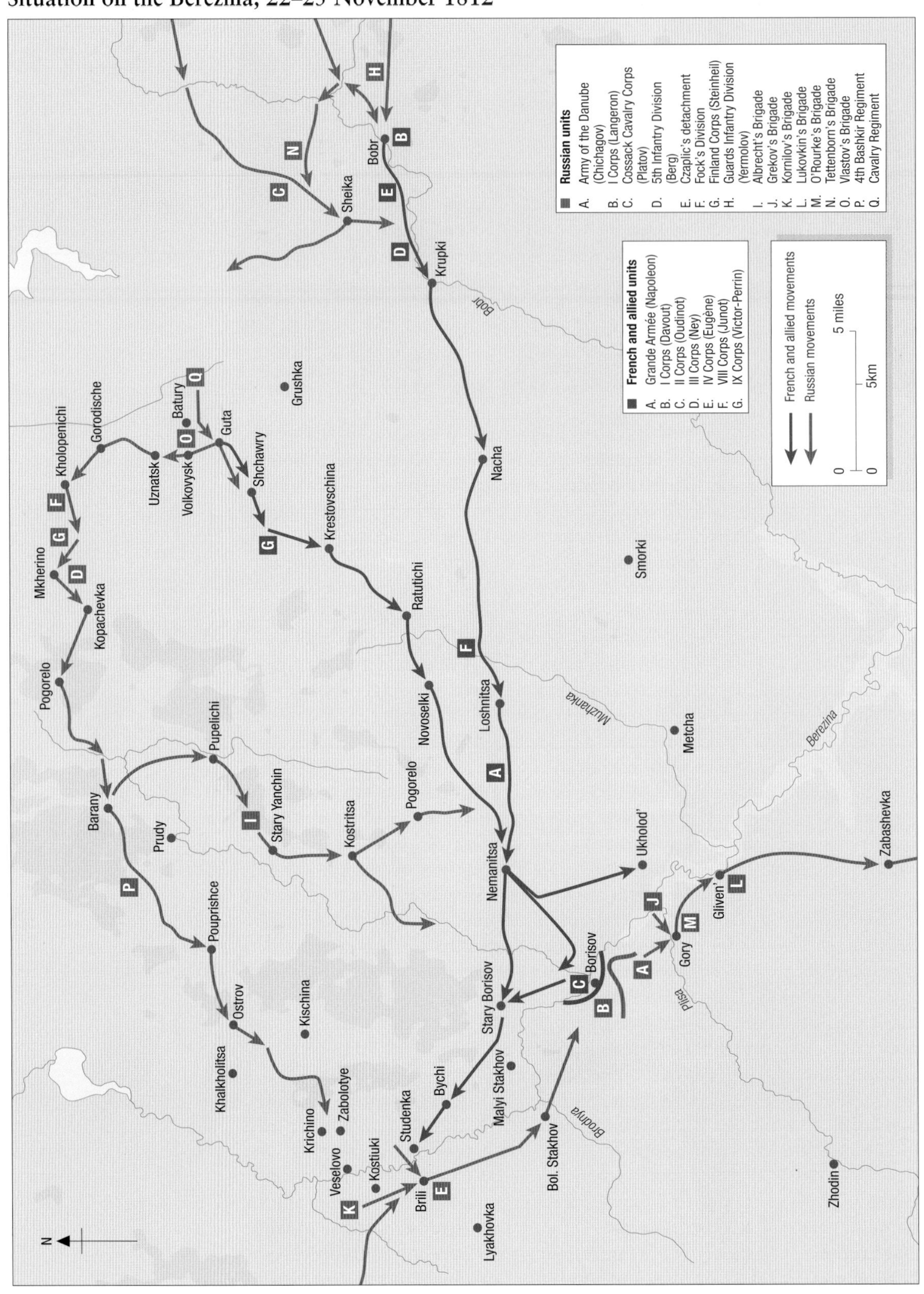

army was still en route, stretched along the western bank; it desperately needed to rest after a fruitless 60-mile march to Berezino and back. Chichagov knew that urgent action was required to prevent Napoleon from escaping. Late that night, he summoned a council of war, which decided to attack the enemy the following morning.

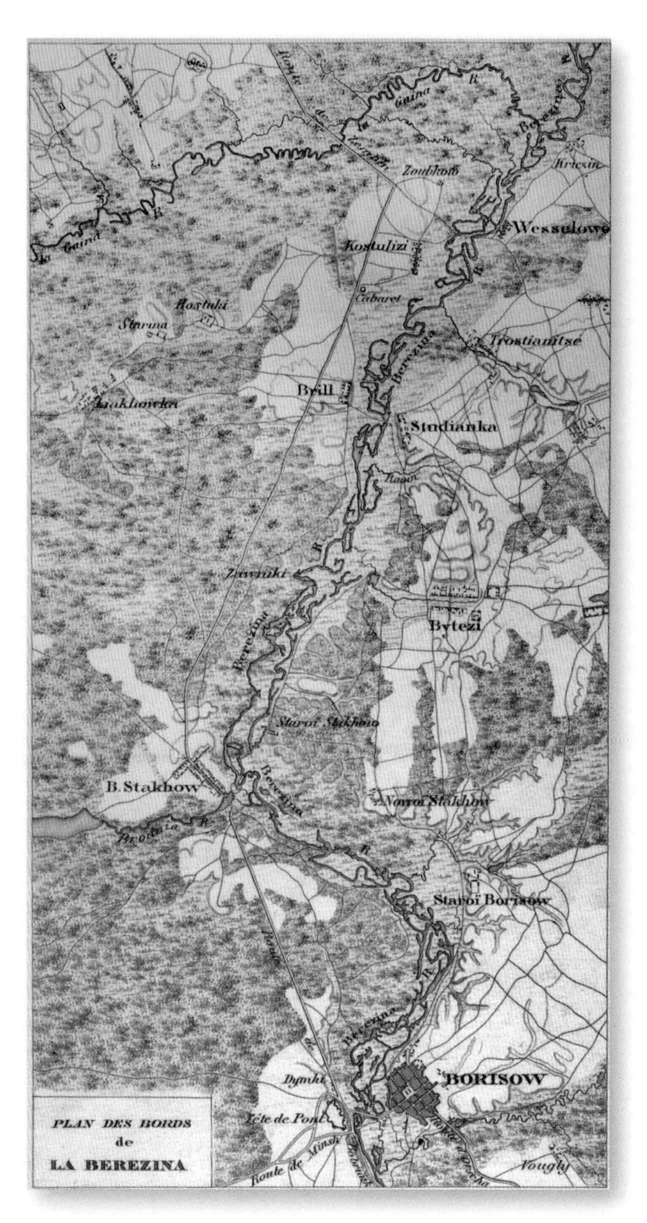

The banks of the Berezina River, from *Atlas de l'Histoire du Consulat et de l'Empire* (1864). (PRISMA ARCHIVO/Alamy)

The Battle of Stary Borisov

The lack of drive in the Russian pursuit enabled Victor's two divisions (Girard's 28th and Daendels' 26th) and Fournier's cavalry to reach Studenka unmolested late in the day while the third, Partouneaux's 12th Division, had stayed behind near Borisov. This division began the campaign with some 12,500 men and 20 guns, but, as Partouneaux pointed out, 'it was made up of young soldiers, many of them refractory conscripts'. During the short campaign in Russia, it lost two-thirds of its roster to 'fatigues, privations and combat' (in the words of Partouneaux) and probably counted some 3,500 men in late November; they were supported by some 500 Saxon and Berg horsemen who were provisionally united into a cavalry brigade. Partouneaux was assisted by three brigade commanders, generals Pierre-Joseph Billard (aged 40), Louis Camus (a veteran of the Revolutionary Wars, whom Partouneaux described as 'a brave man who has performed well in war'), and Marie-Pierre Blanmont (aged 42). The last few weeks of campaigning had made a profound imprint on Partouneaux who was ill and developed war-weariness; in mid-November, Victor-Perrin advised Berthier that the general was 'in such a state that he is unable to continue fighting anymore. In addition to old wounds he had sustained, he has attained a disease which requires immediate rest and assistance.' Partouneaux admitted as much when he appealed to the army's chief of staff to be relieved of his command. 'Until now courage and zeal have kept me going,' he explained, 'but my physical strength has abandoned me; I can no longer stand up to the pains caused by the rigour of the season and my wounds'; his request was ignored and less than two weeks later, this sick and broken man was tasked with protecting the Grande Armée's retreat.

After Victor-Perrin led his two other divisions to Studenka, Partouneaux was instructed to stay at Borisov to delay the Russian advance, prevent the establishment of direct communications between Wittgenstein and Chichagov and protect the stragglers still marching to the crossing site. The defence of Borisov was a vital task during the first two days of the crossing when much of the Grande Armée was still on the eastern bank and vulnerable to attacks from the rear. But the town's importance diminished by 28 November, when most of the army had moved across the Berezina. Yet Partouneaux remained in Borisov. After the war, contemporaries debated whether the 12th Division should have stayed so long and who was at fault for it. Partouneaux defended his actions in a brochure published in 1815, in which he described receiving strict instructions from Berthier to stay put at Borisov through the night of 28 November; his statement was supported by other eyewitnesses, but categorically denied by Napoleon and his apologists. Be that as it may, the delay in departing from Borisov proved fatal for the 12th Division.

Partouneaux spent most of the morning of the 27th waiting for 'immense columns of stragglers' (as he described them) to pass through the town. His men finally entered Borisov around 4pm and rested for one and a half hours to allow the crowds to move on. Dutch Captain Wagevier, who commanded a grenadier company of the 2nd Battalion of the 125th Line, described his troops looking forward to reaching the crossing but feeling exasperated from constant marching and 'falling down from fatigue'. Partouneaux kept Camus' brigade in town and placed the brigades of Billard and Blanmont on the Orsha road to guard the approaches.

By now, Wittgenstein's corps was finally converging on the Grande Armée. Vlastov, who had sent at least two reports advising Wittgenstein of the enemy crossing at Studenka that night, was instructed to lead his 4,000 men and ten cannon to Stary Borisov; he was followed by generals Berg and Steinheil with their respective forces, while Fock remained with the reserves near the village of Kostritsa.

Approaching Stary Borisov, Vlastov encountered the survivors of the Grande Armée marching to the crossing site. He deployed artillery to target the enemy and sent in the replacement battalions of the 11th, 18th and 36th Jäger regiments and two squadrons of the Combined Hussar Regiment, who scattered the enemy crowds and captured hundreds of prisoners. Wittgenstein soon joined Vlastov at Stary Borisov and learned from the prisoners that an entire French division was still at Borisov, effectively cut off from Napoleon's main forces. Delighted to hear this, the Russian commander made preparations for an immediate attack and deployed his troops in strong positions around Stary Borisov. Vlastov's main force was kept north of the village, on the heights overlooking the river; Lieutenant-Colonel Neidhardt, of the Imperial Suite, occupied the village with the Combined Jäger Regiment and a battalion of the 25th Jägers. An artillery battery was deployed behind the settlement while two more light guns, protected by the Sevskii Infantry Regiment and a battalion of the 25th Jägers, were set up next to the main road south of it. Vlastov himself commanded two infantry battalions (with two guns) on what he described as 'an advantageous position' not far from the main road.

The sudden appearance of the Russian troops spread panic among thousands of stragglers moving along the main route. Some of them fled in the direction of Studenka, but others rushed back to Borisov where they cluttered the streets and buildings. Just then, Chichagov attempted to move troops across the repaired bridge at Borisov – the Russian Jägers threw the wooden planks across the damaged sections of the Borisov bridge and rushed into the town. It proved to be a mistake, as Partouneaux's men held their ground and counter-attacked. The 125th Line led the charge, and Captain Wagevier remembered the terrible spectacle that unfolded in front of him:

The Grande Armée continues its retreat after crossing the Berezina. (Kean Collection/ Archive Photos/Getty Images)

'Imagine a place burning brightly and two armies fighting in the midst of it. Burning houses falling in a terrible noise, the thunder of muskets and guns, moans of the wounded and no hope for mercy: the merciless enemy was in front, behind and all around us.' With the Russian Jägers pushed across the river, Partouneaux grasped the gravity of his situation – several miles of woods and swamps separated him from the crossing site, while the enemy troops were threatening his division from both sides of the river. The only way to escape was by forcing a passage.

As the sun set that evening, Partouneaux led his men out of town. Marching in darkness and a blizzard that obscured their vision, the French made a fateful mistake. Not far from Borisov there was a fork where two tracks led northwards. That to the left skirted the riverbank while the one on the right led north-east through Stary Borisov, now occupied by the Russians. With the road to the left already chockfull of stragglers, Partouneaux turned to the right, believing it would take him directly to Studenka: instead, as one participant put it, it took his division 'right into the middle of Wittgenstein's entire corps'; only one battalion, the 4th of the 55th Line, avoided this blunder and reached the bridges by taking the left pathway.

The late-night combat witnessed some most gallant fighting at Stary Borisov as Camus' brigade brushed aside the Russian forward outposts and approached the village; the 44th Line even managed to break into Stary Borisov, where they fought a close-quarter combat with the Russians. But this was the extent of their success – Partouneaux sent in the 3rd Brigade and instructed Blanmont to guard the flank, but in spite of the audacity and determination of their charges, they gained no further ground against a much stronger opponent. By now, Vlastov's forces were reinforced by Steinheil's corps that shored up the Russian centre and left flank; Berg's units formed the reserve. Wittgenstein, thus, had well over 20,000 men and a huge superiority in artillery and cavalry. Moreover, as General Camus later complained, the presence of the throngs of stragglers impeded the French during this battle – 'their crowds mingled among our troops, cluttered the road, and thwarted our manoeuvres'. Amid the fighting, Partouneaux received the distressing news that Russian Colonel Alexander Seslavin's flying detachment, one of the many such units Kutuzov tasked with pursuing the retreating enemy, had raided Borisov and captured thousands of stragglers still remaining there. The loss of Borisov meant that the 12th Division had no place to retreat to and had to fight on two fronts at once. The French general tried scaling the hills on the right and slipping between the Russian units under cover of darkness, but he seems to have failed to clearly convey his intention to his subordinates; after reading Partouneaux's excusatory article in 1821, General Blanmont published a critical response in which he denied receiving any such orders that night. 'I wish I had received the order,' he commented. 'I would have been spared a serious wound and 21 months of captivity.' This criticism stung Partouneaux, who accused his former subordinate of lapsed memory and inability to follow orders.

Late that night, the 12th Division thus found itself scattered around Stary Borisov, its leaders acting disjointedly. Partouneaux rallied several hundred survivors of the 3rd Brigade and sought to break through on the right side but was repelled and driven into half-frozen marshland. Around 11pm, he received another offer to surrender and, casting a dejected look at the cold and utterly spent men still standing by his side, he decided to accept it. Generals Camus and Blanmont, meanwhile, fought on through the night, losing two-thirds of their men. 'It was a veritable butchery!' commented a French participant. To put an end to it, Wittgenstein ordered his men to cease fire and offered terms of surrender. Camus and his officers initially refused to accept it and instead spent a few hours searching in vain for any fords. At dawn, a Russian messenger arrived with the news of the surrender of Partouneaux and the 3rd Brigade. It was clear that further resistance was futile and the remnants of the 12th Division capitulated as well. The number of those killed at Stary Borisov, whether in action or from the elements, remains unknown, but Wittgenstein reported capturing five generals, some 200 officers, and close to 7,000 troops, along with three cannon and two

The surrender of Partouneaux and his brigade at Stary Borisov; a Russian print dated 1814. (Author's collection)

The Grande Armée withdraws over the Berezina. (DeAgostini/ Getty Images)

eagles (of the 44th and 126th Line regiments). Of those taken prisoner, probably only half were from the 12th Division and the rest were stragglers from various units caught up in the fighting.

The victory at Stary Borisov was of double importance for the Russians. Besides the military significance of destroying an enemy division, this success allowed the Russian commanders to establish direct communications with each other. Staff Captain Silvestr Malinovski, serving in Chichagov's headquarters, was elated when he learned of the arrival of the main field army's advance guard, under the command of Ataman Matvei Platov and Major-General Alexei Yermolov, and the construction of the pontoon bridges at Borisov. Important as this development was, it also compounded a problem with which the Russian command had been long grappling. In Kutuzov's absence, Chichagov was senior in rank and, with direct communications established, Wittgenstein was now expected to subordinate himself to him. The proud general, however, felt no inclination to do it. When his messenger reached the headquarters of the Third Western Army, Chichagov discovered that, as he put it, 'Wittgenstein considered himself completely independent and intended to act on his own discretion. Thus, petty vanity interfered and harmed our actions.' Some of Wittgenstein's senior officers were upset by their superior's behaviour and Major-General Ivan Begichev complained that 'we are acting like children who ought to be whipped with birch rods'.

Late in the evening on 28 November, Chichagov held another council of war to plan the next day's attack. He envisioned his army advancing along the western flank and engaging the enemy near Brili and Stakhov; Platov and Yermolov would cross the river at Borisov to support this attack while Wittgenstein's corps was expected to press hard on the eastern side of the river. Chichagov asked Wittgenstein to send reinforcements, but the general did not respond to the request and only offered a vague promise to attack at dawn. That same evening, Kutuzov's messenger arrived with the latest dispatches from the Main Army. The news was discouraging: the supreme commander was still six marches away. 'This shows how "relentlessly" Kutuzov was pursuing the enemy,' Chichagov remarked scornfully. 'It is called 'biting at the enemy's heels from a reasonable distance".'

DAY THREE: 28 NOVEMBER 1812

The dawn of the new day was cold, windy and overcast. Passing through Borisov, one of Chichagov's messengers complained that 'all roads were covered with snow; crowds of stragglers were wandering in nearby fields, setting up fires, slicing horse cadavers, gnawing at bones, frying or eating raw meat ... The road was lined with the bodies of dead soldiers and horses, showing me the way forward'.

With the convergence of the Russian forces, Napoleon found himself in a dire predicament. Chichagov had some 30,000 men, Wittgenstein had 35,000–38,000, and Yermolov and Platov brought 12,000 more, which meant that the Russians could rally some 75,000 men near the crossing site. Yet petty rivalries and poor coordination hampered the Russian war effort. The effective strength of Chichagov's forces committed to the attack on the western bank was around 23,000–25,000 men while Wittgenstein diverted only 15,000 men to Studenka, keeping the rest at Stary Borisov and Borisov; Platov guarded the Minsk road and Yermolov's detachment (dog-tired after a forced march) was kept in reserve. Thus, the effective strength of the Russian forces engaged in the battles of 28 November probably reached 40,000. Chichagov wanted to move part of the cavalry, especially the ever-mobile Cossacks, to the left flank, where they could break through to the Zembino swamps and destroy the wooden causeways to cut Napoleon's line of retreat. However, to accomplish this, the cavalry first had to cross the Gaina River, which was not frozen yet and, though shallow, was surrounded with impassable swamps. Thus, the plan did not work.

The Battle of Brili/Stakhov

As the first sunrays pierced the cold morning air, the Russian forces were on the move on the western bank. Czaplic deployed his forces in four groups: Major-General Rudzevich led the 12th and 22nd Jägers in the centre, supported by Major-General Kornilov's 32nd and 28th Jägers on the right and Major-General Mesherinov's 7th and 27th Jägers in the woods on the left; Arnoldi's 13th Horse Artillery Company and three battery companies (9th, 18th and 38th) moved along the main road, under protection of the

The crossing of the Berezina, by January Suchodolski. (Public Domain)

The Grande Armée troops, with throngs of stragglers, crossing the Berezina during Wittgenstein's attack, a detail from a watercolour attributed to François Fournier-Sarloveze. (DeAgostini/Getty Images)

Pavlogradskii hussars; Colonel A. Krasovskii's 14th Jägers formed the extreme right flank that was adjacent to the river. Chichagov formed the reserves with the 9th and 18th divisions, which he placed under the command of General Sabaneyev.

The western bank of the Berezina was covered in thick forest but these were trees without undergrowth and not very close together, over most of the ground. On such a field there was little scope for the use of cavalry and artillery. Anticipating the enemy assaults, Napoleon made excellent dispositions for battle, deploying his forces in a deep defensive position. The first line included Oudinot's II Corps: Maison's 8th Division was on the left side of the road, Legrand (6th Division) in the centre, and Merle (9th Division) on the right; a thick chain of skirmishers was deployed in front of them. Behind them was the second defensive line, commanded by Marshal Ney; in the centre, along the main road, stood the remaining survivors of the III and V corps; the 17th Division was on the left side, while the Vistula Legion held the right flank. A few hundred yards behind them was the third line, comprised of Doumerc's cuirassiers and the light cavalry brigades of Castex and Corbineau. Further behind was Napoleon's main reserve – Mortier's Young Guard, Lefevbre's Old Guard and Bessières' Guard Cavalry – that protected the I and IV corps as they accompanied transports, wounded and stragglers to the Zembino marshes. Victor's IX Corps was still on the eastern bank, where a vast multitude of stragglers gathered, probably as many as 15,000. The strength of Napoleon's army is impossible to determine with precision but it could not have numbered more than 30,000, two-thirds of them already on the western bank. That morning, Jacob Anthony Tellegen of the 128th Line and his comrades tried to gage their prospects, but judged their situation very grave – 'starving, shivering with cold, facing an enemy ten times stronger than us'. Not far from them Marshal Oudinot gathered his staff officers for a meagre breakfast, where everyone had to contribute

1
1

THE SWISS SAVE THE DAY, 28 NOVEMBER 1812 (PP. 66–67)

Here, early in the morning of 28 November, the battle is raging on the west bank of the Berezina to protect the bridges from the attacking Russian troops. A group of Swiss soldiers from the 1st Swiss Regiment (**1**) are charging from the woods. The Swiss drummers were reluctant to beat the attack, so Lieutenant Thomas Legler (**2**) of the 1st Swiss Regiment has seized a drummer – a Swiss lad by the name of Kundert (**3**) – by his collar and is dragging Kundert behind him to the front line, while Kundert beats the attack with one hand.

As the 1st Swiss Regiment were preparing to enter the fray, Commandant Blattmann had asked Lieutenant Legler to sing his favourite song, *Unser Leben gleicht der Reise* (*Our Life is but a Journey*). 'I started to sing at once,' Legler recalled later, 'and when I finished, Blattmann heaved a deep sigh, "Yes, Legler, that is how it is! Such splendid words!"' Other officers and soldiers took up singing and marched straight into the fray:

Our life is but a journey
Of a pilgrim through the night;
Everyone faces on their path
Much that causes grief.

But suddenly the night and darkness
Dissipate before us,
And the troubled find
Relief from their suffering.

So let us march forward!
Do not yield to despair!
Beyond those distant heights
Good fortune still awaits us.

Be brave, be brave, beloved brothers!
Cast all concerns aside!
The sun will rise again tomorrow
Lifting our hopes high up into the sky.

Among the units supporting Merle's Swiss infantry regiments were a squadron of Polish lancers (**4**). The memoirs of Jean-Marc Bussy, a soldier of the 3rd Swiss Regiment, provide additional details on the Swiss participation: 'We fought for a long time without gaining any ground. It seemed to us that the enemy was receiving reinforcements since his fire intensified … Suddenly, we were pushed back for some 50 steps. Then our chiefs shouted: "*En avant!*" The charge overwhelmed the enemy … who withdrew slowly and kept firing. Soon our advance was checked by the charging enemy cavalry … Our battery and that of the 4th Regiment destroyed the Russian battery, which was then abandoned on the road.'

something; some supplied breadcrumbs, others onions and a lump of lard. They were about to partake in their paltry meal when, around 7am, the news arrived of the enemy attack.

The Russians initially gained some ground, driving the French skirmishers back. But they soon encountered a major impediment. Marching on both sides of the road, they had to navigate through dense forest that prevented them from maintaining battle formations or deploying their artillery batteries. Czaplic was compelled to let his men fight in open order even though he and other Russian generals knew that the French were more experienced at skirmishing and, in the words of Langeron, 'were more accustomed to acting independently'. The combat was, thus, obstinate and bloody.

Around 8am, Oudinot counter-attacked with Merle's division, the Swiss infantry marching at its head. The four Swiss regiments must have numbered about 2,500 men and were supported by a few Polish infantry, chasseurs and lancers. The men narrowed their eyes and inclined their bodies forward, like men in heavy rain, and charged on. They fought fiercely until exhausting their cartridges; several messengers dispatched to get ammunition were either killed or wounded amid murderous firing. Legler witnessed dozens of officers being wounded and killed, including Blattmann who was shot in the head; a round shot cleaved off the head of General Candras' adjutant. Taking cover behind the trees, soldiers responded to officers' orders to fight on by saying 'Give us cartridges!' Legler urged the drummers to lead the attack, but they all refused it. So, in the heat of the moment, he seized one of the drummers – a Swiss lad by the name of Kundert from the Glarus canton – by his collar and threatened to run his sword through him if he did not follow at once. Legler rushed forward, with Kundert beating the attack, and the Swiss infantry, moved by their example, charged with bayonets fixed. The Swiss attack lasted a few minutes before it was swept up in the Russian counter-attack, with Legler and his comrades finding themselves in a close melee with the enemy cavalry. The savagery of the fighting that raged in those woods can be seen from the fact that less than two dozen men, and just two officers, survived from the entire 2nd Swiss Regiment. Jean-Marc Bussy, a soldier of the 3rd Swiss Regiment, thought his regiment charged over half a dozen times, and each time it covered the ground with dead and wounded.

Under pressure from superior Russian forces, the II Corps began to give way. Oudinot did his best to rally his men, but there were not many of them left. The 123rd Line, a few dozen men strong, was tasked with supporting the Swiss and holding up the left flank. D'Auzon de Boisminart, commanding the regimental artillery of the 124th

The charge of the Swiss troops at the Berezina, by Karl Jauslin. (Swiss National Museum)

FRENCH AND ALLIED

A. 9th Division: Merle (acting division commander – François-Pierre-Joseph Amey)
Brigade Amey: 4th Swiss Regiment, 3rd Croatian Regiment (remnants of two battalions mauled at Polotsk)
Brigade Candras: 1st Swiss Regiment, 2nd Swiss Regiment
Brigade Coutard: 123rd Line Infantry Regiment, 3rd Swiss Regiment
Artillery: 4th/7th Foot Artillery; 5th/2nd Horse Artillery

B. 6th Division: Legrand
26th Light Infantry Regiment and 19th Infantry Regiment

C. 8th Division: Maison
Brigade Viviès: 11th Light Infantry Regiment (four battalions), 2nd Line Infantry Regiment (five battalions)
Brigade Pouget (wounded, not present): 37th Line Infantry Regiment (four battalions), 124th (Dutch) Line Infantry Regiment (three battalions)
Artillery: 15th/5th Foot Artillery (eight guns); 1st/3rd Horse Artillery (six guns)

D. The Vistula (Polish) Legion: Michel-Marie Claparède
1st, 2nd and 3rd Infantry regiments

The Polish V Corps: General Józef Zajączek:

E. Remnants of the 16th (Zajączek) and 18th divisions (Karol Kniaziewicz)
2nd, 3rd, 8th, 12th, 15th and 16th Polish regiments

F. 17th Infantry Division – General Jan Henryk Dąbrowski
1st, 6th, 10th, 14th and 17th Polish regiments

General Jean-Pierre Doumerc's Cavalry

G. 7th Cuirassier Regiment
H. 4th Cuirassier Regiment

Remnants of the 4th Cavalry Corps (Dziewanowski's Polish lancers)

I. 2nd Polish Lancer Regiment
J. 7th Polish Lancer Regiment
K. 15th Polish Lancer Regiment

Other

L. The Young Guard
M. The Old Guard
N. Napoleon and his staff
O. The Imperial Guard Cavalry
P. Grande Armée units marching away from the Berezina River
Q. Napoleon's initial headquarters at the village of Zanivki

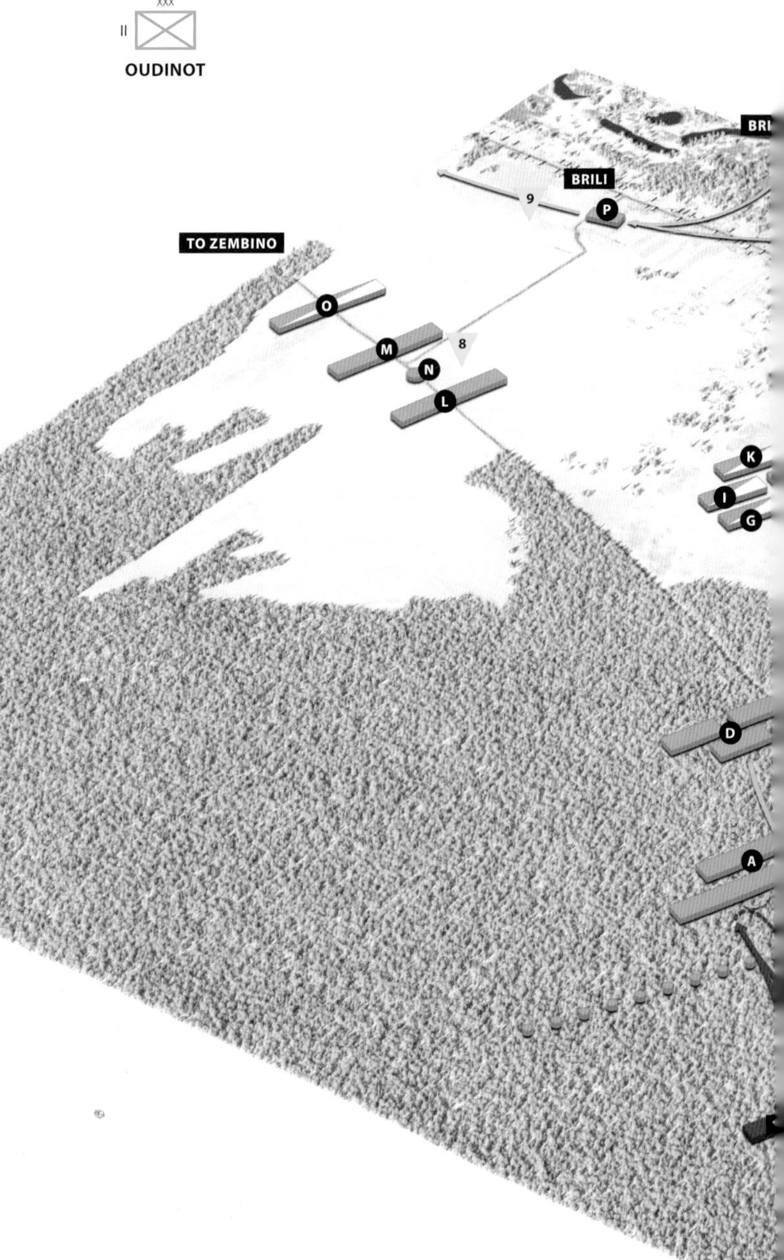

EVENTS

1. The Russian attack commences around 7am, with Czaplic's advance guard leading the charge. The Russians drive the enemy skirmishers back but are unable to penetrate Marshal Oudinot's main position.

2. Oudinot counter-attacks with Merle's division, the Swiss infantry marching, and singing, at its head. The Dutch regiments advance on their left flank. The vicious and confused fighting rages for over an hour, with losses mounting on both sides. Many senior officers are killed and wounded; Oudinot is injured and carried to the rear. Napoleon orders Ney to take charge.

3. Ney rallies the II Corps and calls up the Vistula Legion and the remnants of the V Corps to contain the Russian advance.

4. Late in the morning, Sabaneyev arrives with reinforcements, 18th Division; some regiments are deployed in open order, scattered over a large area inside the woods, where the Russian commanders (Inzov on the left and Sherbatov on the right) are unable to exercise effective control.

5. Ney notices the Russian mistake and orders the cuirassier and lancer regiments to attack. Doumerc's 4th, 7th and 14th Cuirassier regiments, supported by Dziewanowski's Polish lancers (2nd, 7th and 15th regiments) charge through the woods and wreak havoc on the exposed Russian infantry, which falls back and spreads confusion among other units.

6. Sabaneyev rushes forward the 9th Division to shore up the Russian front line and gains enough time for his subordinates to rally their main units. The Russian cavalry counter-charges the French; the fighting is at close quarters, fast and unforgiving.

7. Sabaneyev renews the assault, with the Russian infantry regiments launching several attacks, all of them unsuccessful. Ney's French, Swiss, Dutch and Polish infantry hold the ground for the rest of the day.

8. Napoleon remains with the Imperial Guard throughout the day but on at least one occasion he travels closer to the front line to observe the fighting. He remains reluctant to commit the Guard.

9. As the battle rages, units and stragglers continue to cross the Berezina and march towards Zembino.

THE BEREZINA: WEST OF THE RIVER, 28 NOVEMBER

Having realized the actual location of Napoleon's crossing, Chichagov directed half of his army to intercept the Grande Armée. Marshal Nicolas-Charles Oudinot's II Corps, supported by the V (Polish) Corps and the cuirassier and lancer regiments, fought fiercely to contain the Russian advance on the outskirts of Brili and to allow the rest of the Grande Armée to escape.

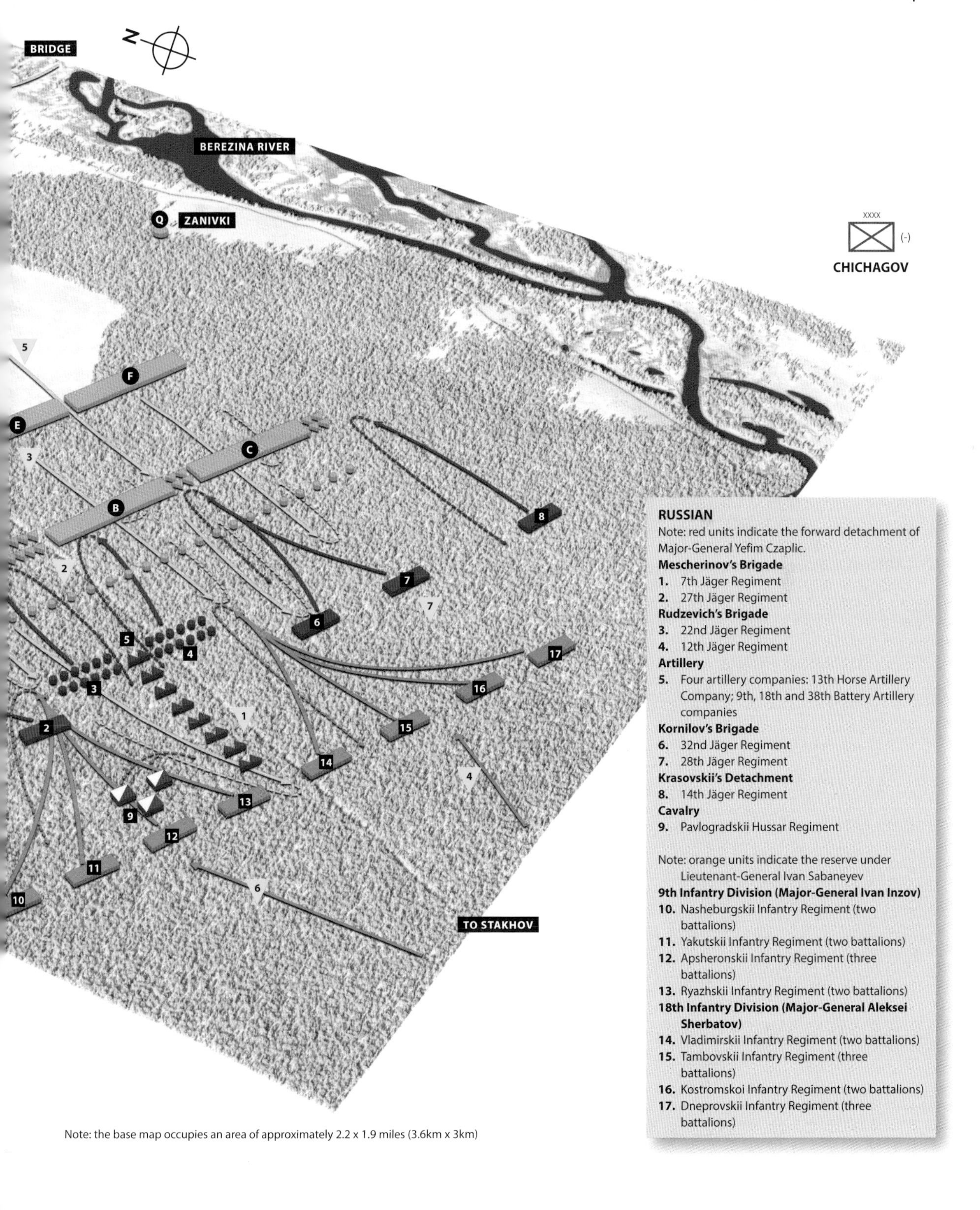

Note: the base map occupies an area of approximately 2.2 x 1.9 miles (3.6km x 3km)

Marshal Ney during the retreat from Russia, by the artist Ruhiere. (The Print Collector/ Getty Images)

Line, recalled that only about 100 men were still standing in his regiment; all officers massed together while the '*peloton de l'Aigle*', led by Lieutenant-Colonel Mouchet, was moved to the rear to avoid the loss of the eagle. After the colonel of the 56th Line was killed, Tellegen, who was already tasked with leading the 128th Line, had to take command of this regiment as well. 'The blade of my sword was shot in half and several bullets pierced my clothes,' he remembered. Not long after taking on his new command, a spent bullet struck him in the chest and broke two ribs. Forced to leave the front line, Tellegen came across Oudinot, who gave instructions to his last surviving aide-de-camp. Just then, the marshal was hit by a shell splinter – his 22nd wound – and fell from the saddle; his foot, however, was caught in the stirrup and the startled horse dragged him with his head on the ground for some distance. Men rushed to the marshal's aid and carried him into the woods, where they prepared a stretcher out of pine branches. Just then, Napoleon reached an opening in the woods in time to see the wounded Oudinot being carried off. He sent his physicians to tend him and put Ney in command of Oudinot's forces with strict orders to hold the Russians at all costs.

The emperor's messenger found the 'Bravest of the Brave' atop a little white horse a few hundred yards from the front line; each time a round shot whistled over, he shouted, 'Keep flying past, rascals!' Following Napoleon's order, Ney rallied II Corps and, calling up his own troops and those of the Vistula Legion and the V Corps, he checked Czaplic's advance. The sound of revived battle resonated through the woods. The Polish infantry, led by General Józef Zajączek who was assisted by Dąbrowski and Karol Kniaziewicz, advanced on both sides of the road and charged with such élan that it pushed the Russians back for some distance. Captain Ignacy Prądzyński, a staff officer under Dąbrowski, watched as the columns of his comrades moved forward. 'Because of the undergrowth and the fallen trees, they had to break formation and became mixed up with the soldiers of the enemy. Not being able to fire volleys, both sides tried to shoot at point-blank range, but the falling snow made the muskets unserviceable, so both sides resorted to bayonets and musket butts.'

Alarmed by the tottering of his battle line, Chichagov ordered Sabaneyev to move the 18th Infantry Division out of the reserve and reinforce the front line. Sabaneyev, who had spent much of his career in the light infantry units, committed a momentous mistake in the first minutes of the attack when he ordered most of the division to deploy in open order. The newly arriving units spread out over a large area inside the woods and the Russian commanders soon found themselves unable to exercise effective control over many of them; command, control, manoeuvre and communication were lost in the shadows of the forest. Czaplic, who eagerly expected the reinforcements, was 'bewildered to hear drums beating and see troops spreading as skirmishers'. He rushed to see whom these were and urged local commanders to recall their troops and form columns at once, but they refused to comply because of 'existing orders' from their superiors. Exasperated, Czaplic galloped to General Voinov, informing him 'about disadvantages resulting from such inept directives', Voinov simply shrugged his shoulders, pointing to Sabaneyev as the source for these instructions. Unable to get Sabaneyev to change his mind and seething with anger, Czaplic returned to his troops.

By then, Marshal Ney had noticed the mistake in the Russian disposition, and moved to exploit it at once. He ordered General Doumerc to advance with his cuirassier regiments (4th, 7th and 14th, up to 400 men in total), supported by Dziewanowski's Polish lancers (2nd, 7th and 15th, some 700 men). Despite popular perception, the cuirassiers were not entirely French and the 14th Cuirassiers, in fact, consisted of the Dutch horsemen led by Colonel Albert Dominicus Trip van Zoudtlandt, who would later distinguish himself fighting the French at Waterloo. The cavalrymen quickly moved up to the front line where, as Marbot pointed out, the forest was sparser and the cavalry could move between the trees. Thomas Legler, who was desperately rallying the survivors of his 1st Swiss Regiment, was delighted to see 'the brave cuirassiers of the 4th and 7th regiments' lining up close to the road. He soon heard the word of command, 'Squadrons, by the left flank, march!' and the cuirassiers went into the attack.

Doumerc's charge wrought havoc on the Russian infantrymen. His 'iron men' and the Polish lancers rode down the dispersed Russian units, which were entirely surprised by this ferocious attack; Langeron described the cuirassiers emerging from between the trees and undergrowth, joining other cuirassiers at the edge of two small plains, forming up in a flash and charging. As they fled, the Russian soldiers spread further confusion among their comrades in the rear, which allowed the French and their allies to gain ground; Doumerc later praised the 14th Cuirassiers for 'making successive charges' that prevented the Russian infantry from reforming.

Major-General Lieders rushed his 9th Division forward and gained enough time for Czaplic and Sherbatov to rally their men; the Russian cavalry soon arrived as well, with the St Petersburgskii, Kinburgskii, Starodubskii and Tverskii dragoons counter-charging the French cuirassiers and Polish lancers. The fighting was at close quarters, fast and furious. Jean-Marc Bussy, from the 3rd Swiss, remembered:

> We cannot fire with so many troops intermingling. So a bayonet and the butt of the rifle are used to parry and deliver blows ... We still manage to gain considerable ground but cannot regain our initial position. We can see men lying on the snow and realize that our ranks have been depleted while the enemy is receiving reinforcements. It is with our resolve that we must compensate for numbers ... The fighting is worse than butchery. There is blood everywhere on the snow, which is beaten up by constant advancing and retreating ... One no longer dares to look on the right or left, fearing not to see his friend, his comrade any longer. Our ranks are tightening, our line shortening, our courage redoubles. We fight a little more closely, charging with bayonets. Terrible clash, which we sustain with unusual intrepidity. Horrible carnage! To get to the bridges, the enemy must pass through us first, but we fight to the last!

14
7

THE CHARGE OF DOUMERC'S 'MEN OF IRON', 28 NOVEMBER 1812 (PP. 74–75)

In this scene, a group of French 14th Cuirassiers (**1**) are charging through the woods towards the dispersed Russian infantry from the 9th and 18th divisions (**2**, plus 7th Jägers from the 8th Division), which are hastily falling back. Some cuirassiers are slashing at their foes, others galloping at full speed.

Fighting between trees, over and through bushes, in between and under horses, made it difficult for one to distinguish friend or foe. As the cavalry burst through the woods, a Russian soldier, isolated from his regiment, had little time to think but could only trust that his training would not fail him. Amid the chaotic scenes of fighting, many Russian officers were killed, wounded or captured; Czaplic was wounded, Voinov got bruised falling after his horse was killed, while General Sherbatov was almost captured, saved only by the timely arrival of the Russian hussars. The French cavalry charge, Czaplic acknowledged in his memoirs, had 'a devastating effect on us, especially since the soldiers [of the 18th Division] who were supposed to support me, became scattered in the woods and, in the confusion, began firing in my rear so I found myself caught in crossfire, which only further increased confusion among our troops.' Rochechouart, leading two grenadier battalions to secure a spot in the woods, was stunned to see three cuirassier squadrons galloping through the forest – 'they sabred and put to rout our grenadiers'. Yermolov could not see 'a clearing in the woods where enemy cuirassier detachments did not attack and disorganize our infantry'.

After recalling his horsemen, Doumerc deployed cuirassier squadrons behind infantry regiments and occasionally counter-attacked through the intervals between the Polish and Swiss units; Lieutenant Wincenty Placzkowski of the Polish lancers of the Imperial Guard, recalled hearing Napoleon's orders for 'one company from each regiment of infantry and cavalry of the Guard to be detached'. The arrival of these veteran soldiers steadied the front line. The fighting was largely conducted inside the woods and was chaotic, which complicates its precise reconstruction. The Russian regimental histories reveal that both sides exchanged repeated attacks. The Kostromskoi, Tambovskii and Apsheronskii regiments made several charges only to be repelled and counter-attacked in turn; the latter unit alone withstood four major cavalry charges, losing some 100 killed and wounded. On the opposite side, the Swiss, Dutch and Polish infantry held ground throughout the day and the French and Polish artillery performed exceptionally well; Czaplic complained about the 'hellish fire' of the enemy cannon that 'devastated everything' and sent 'splinters flying everywhere, which inflicted serious injuries on our men'. Langeron agreed: 'The fire of these guns was so continual and so devastating that it became very difficult for generals and their aides-de-camp to cross the road without exposing themselves to a great danger.'

In the afternoon, Wittgenstein, who had earlier promised to send reinforcements, crossed the river to see Chichagov in person. The admiral was not at all amused to see the general arrive alone, without any troops, around 2pm. He outlined the situation and again asked for reinforcements, but Wittgenstein demurred. 'What do you intend to do now?' he wondered. 'The enemy would keep fighting until darkness and would then, as usual, retreat.' Such indifference exasperated Chichagov, who lambasted Wittgenstein for returning to Borisov and 'indifferently' observing the battle from afar. 'After promising me to advance at the same time as we did at 5am,' the admiral wrote in his memoirs, 'Wittgenstein launched his attack only at 10am and even then failed to get Victor out of his positions for the entire day. He committed only 14,000 men and refused to reinforce me with two divisions.

The heroism of the Dutch troops holding their ground on the western bank of the Berezina, as envisioned by the Dutch painter Jan Hoynck van Papendrecht. (Author's collection)

The Swiss monument to troops who fell at the Berezina, erected in Studenka (Studianka, Belarus). (Alain Poirot/Alamy)

And so, most of his forces stood idle at a distance.'

The fighting on the western bank continued until sunset when it gradually died down amidst the fast-approaching darkness. Oudinot's corps lost up to 5,000 men that day, but as the survivors prepared for the night, their shattered ranks still held their own and their courage and devotion saved the rest of the army. Still, the losses were heavy. Many Allied generals and senior officers were wounded. General Canderas was killed, while generals Legrand, Dąbrowski, Zajączek, Claparède, Kniaziewicz, Albert, Amey, Moreau and Groigne were wounded. The Swiss regiments, which listed up to 4,000 men in the days before, now counted barely one-tenth of that; the 2nd Swiss had been virtually destroyed. Bussy's company had 87 voltigeurs before the battle – 'today, only seven of us are healthy and sound'. The Poles suffered equally grievously; the 15th Polish Regiment lost half its strength while the 14th Regiment over one-third. Hundreds of wounded were abandoned on the battlefield and froze to death during the cold night.

The lion's share of fighting was done by non-French forces, mainly Swiss, Dutch and Poles. Their role, however, was often overlooked, their accomplishment subsumed under the all-encompassing 'French' label. Swiss veteran Jean-Pierre Maillard justly complained that 'our beautiful regiments were destroyed that day but few histories mention this'. Reading Adolphe Thiers' famous *Histoire du Consulate et de l'Empire*, many Polish officers could not hide their indignation at the fact that his account of the Berezina crossing failed to mention Polish contributions. Andrzej Daleki, of the 9th Polish Regiment, expressed the frustration of many Polish participants when he commented that 'wherever the French faced difficulties, they invariably sent us, the Poles, to resolve them – when it was necessary to lead the attack, we were sent ahead; when the army had to retreat, we were placed in the rear to cover it'. Captain Prot Lelewel bewailed the countless Polish casualties 'for whom there will be no mention and no memory! Yet it was due to such sacrifices that the army maintained its position on the Berezina until nightfall.'

The Battle of Studenka

Meanwhile on the eastern bank, Victor's IX Corps fought with equal heroism and success. On 27 November, the marshal received imperial orders instructing him to occupy a strong position on the heights in front of Studenka and guard the approaches to the bridges. 'We did not sleep that night,' remembered Captain Józef Rudnicki of the 4th Polish Regiment. 'We calmly lay down on the bare ground despite the heavy frost ... we only had our thin tunics or greatcoats for protection.' Victor's corps had been greatly weakened by the loss of Partouneaux's division and could hardly expect to hold out against Wittgenstein's corps; most of its artillery and the Baden brigade were already across river. Early in the morning of 28 November, Napoleon therefore ordered the Badenese infantry (Daendels' division) to move back, but deemed it too dangerous to send back the artillery considering the precariousness of the transport bridge; instead he set up a strong battery on the right bank to protect Victor's right flank that was anchored on the shoreline.

In anticipation of the Russian attack, Victor took the rising ground, just south of Studenka. The position sat across the road that ran from the village to Borisov and protected the marshy stream running into the Berezina; the infantry stayed behind the crest that was occupied by a line of skirmishers. On the right, close to the river, there was a cluster of trees defended by Hochberg's Badenese Brigade (1st and 3rd regiments, Baden Jäger Battalion, with six cannon), supported by the 4th Battalion of the 55th Line, whose 213 men were the sole survivors from Partouneaux's division. Next on the left stood General Damas' Berg Brigade (1st, 2nd, 3rd and 4th regiments), followed by Girard's 4th, 7th and 9th Polish regiments, with Löw's Saxon brigade in support. On the extreme left flank, Victor placed General Fournier with 400 or so surviving horsemen from the Baden Hussars and Hesse-Darmstadt Chevau-légers. All in all, the French marshal commanded about 7,000 men and 15 cannon.

After accepting Partouneaux's surrender that morning, Wittgenstein ordered Steinheil to disarm and guard the prisoners, and commanded the rest of the corps to storm Studenka. Vlastov's advance guard – 23rd and 25th Jägers, Combined Jäger Battalion, Combined Hussar Regiment, and Cossacks, about 4,000 men with 12 cannon – spearheaded this advance

Crossing the Berezina River, by Peter Heinrich Lambert von Hess. (Fine Art Images/Heritage Images/Getty Images)

while Lieutenant-General Berg and Major-General Fock, with some 12,000 soldiers, were not far behind it; Wittgenstein himself remained at Borisov.

The weather was worsening; Lieutenant-General Berg complained about the strong wind that whipped up snow flurries and blinded the advancing Russian soldiers. Around 9am, Vlastov's men engaged Victor's outposts near the village of Bychi and pushed them back to Studenka, where they observed the IX Corps deployed along the distant ridge on the southern side of the village. After reconnoitring the enemy position, Vlastov sent his hussars and Cossacks, under command of Colonel Rodion von Gerngross, to turn the French left flank, but these were met by Fournier's cavalrymen. Undaunted, Vlastov switched to the right, dispatching the 23rd Jägers to secure the small patch of woods bordering the river and thus threatening to cut off Victor from the bridges. To support this attack, the Russian general had his 12 cannon (from 1st Horse Artillery Corps and 28th Battery Company) deployed on the knoll and started shelling Victor's position and the area behind it.

The Russian cannonade caused indescribable panic and confusion amidst the vast throngs of people still remaining on the eastern bank. As soon as the sound of gunfire was heard, everyone rushed toward the bridges' narrow approaches, where, driven by the instinct of self-preservation, people fought their way forward by any and every means. Labaume witnessed dreadful scenes of human callousness and misery as 'many perished by mutual slaughter' and 'a greater number still was suffocated towards the entrance to the bridge'. The terrified and desperate crowd behaved 'like an angry sea continually engulfing fresh victims'; the sick, the wounded, women and children were trodden down or forced remorselessly into the river; some committed suicide to hasten the end, others slipped up and fell into the freezing water and kept crying out with their strength for rescue; none was forthcoming. Rudnicki, wounded and carried by his comrades on their muskets, watched in anguish as some men gambled on crossing the river on horseback. To their misfortune, the thin ice invariably gave way under their weight and 'the Berezina welcomed rider and horse into the abyss'.

The survivors huddled in a confused and densely packed mass more than 200 paces deep. Commissaire des guerres Alexandre Bellot de Kergorre was

Monument by sculptor Ivan Misko commemorating the French soldiers who fell at the Berezina, located on the path crossing the Brili marshes, opposite Studenka village. (Alain Poirot/Alamy)

aghast when he saw the footbridge ringed around by a semi-circle of corpses several layers high. 'One could not afford to make a false step because once you had fallen, the man behind you would put his foot on your stomach and you would add yourself to the number of the dying.' To complicate matters even more, around 10am, the transport bridge broke under the weight of carriages and wagons. The crowd naturally rushed to the other bridge, where it became impossible to squeeze through as, in Bourgogne's words, 'everyone mingled in frightful disorder'. In the midst of this chaos, the engineers, pontonniers and sappers were still faithfully at work repairing the broken trestles and sacrificing their lives to save others. Eblé tried in vain to establish a little order; placing himself at the head of the bridge, he kept shouting at the swarm of people but to no avail. This mass of people was utterly unmanageable.

In the meantime, on the outskirts of Studenka, the battle raged on. The ground that Vlastov's men gained on Victor's right wing proved untenable as Napoleon directed the battery, established on the western riverbank, to target the exposed Russian troops. This allowed the Badenese Brigade, commanded by the 20-year-old Count Wilhelm von Hochberg, the future Margrave of Baden, to reoccupy its initial position and hold it for the rest of the day against incessant assaults. Much the same happened on the opposite flank, where Vlastov's cavalry gained temporary success before being driven back by Fournier's men. Exasperated, Vlastov deployed his main forces across the road and set up strong batteries to bombard the French positions. By noon, Victor's corps was already suffering considerable losses and Captain von Zech could see 'gaps opening in the position'. To suppress this fire and gain time to regroup, Victor ordered Damas to charge with his Berg Brigade, which engaged the Russian jägers and drove them back a few hundred paces.

Just then, however, the first units of Lieutenant-General Berg's detachment began to arrive. 'Around 10am I was already opposite the enemy's position,' remembered Berg. 'I immediately ordered strong batteries with two dozen cannon set up to target the enemy and, amidst the most violent cannonade waged from both sides, I began deploying my troops.' Receiving Vlastov's urgent messages requesting succour, Berg dispatched the 24th Jägers to contain Damas' attack; he then shored up the Russian position by deploying the Permskii Infantry Regiment atop a hill in the centre and moved the rest of his forces – the Sevskii Infantry Regiment, the 10th *druzhina* of the St Petersburg Militia, the 4th *druzhina* of the Novgorod Militia, and the 1st Marine Regiment – to the left; a battery of 12 heavy cannon was set up to batter the advancing enemy troops. These reinforcements halted the attack of the Berg Brigade, which suffered greatly from the Russian canister and musket fire (Damas was wounded in the chest) and was forced to retreat.

Soon thereafter came Major-General Fock with another 6,000 men and 36 cannon, which deployed on the right side of the road. Victor's men were now outnumbered 2:1 but fought on with magnificent tenacity and vigour. 'The Russians repeatedly attacked us under the cover of some intensive artillery fire,' described Rudnicki. 'By noon the fields around us were already covered with dead.'

In the early afternoon, Vlastov and Fock commenced another major attack, with the Nizovskii and Voronezhskii Infantry regiments (each one battalion strong) at the lead. This was the crucial moment of the battle as the Russians crossed the stream, scaled the hills, and threatened to penetrate

FRENCH AND ALLIED

Note: The secondary dispositions of Victor's units, having pulled back to the Berezina River, are shown in a lighter shade of blue.

26th Division (General of Division Herman Willem Daendels)

The Badenese Brigade of Wilhelm Graf von Hochberg, Markgraf und Prinz von Baden:

A. 4th Battalion of the 55th Regiment
B. 1st Baden Regiment
C. Baden Light Infantry Battalion
D. 3rd Baden Regiment

The Berg Brigade of General of Brigade François-Étienne Damas:

E. 1st Berg Regiment (two battalions)
F. 4th Berg Regiment (two battalions)
G. 3rd Berg Regiment (one battalion)
H. 2nd Berg Regiment (two battalions)

28th Division (General of Division Jean-Baptiste Girard)

Polish Brigade of General of Brigade Édouard Żółtowski:

I. 4th Polish Regiment (two battalions)
J. A company of sappers
K. 7th Polish Regiment (two battalions)
L. 9th Polish Regiment (two battalions)

Saxon Brigade (General of Brigade Claude-Louis de Villiers)

M. Saxon Regiment von Low (two battalions)
N. Saxon Regiment von Rechten (two battalions)

Cavalry (General of Division François Fournier-Sarlovèze)

O. Baden Hussar Regiment (four squadrons)
P. Hesse-Darmstadt Light Cavalry (four squadrons)

Other

Q. The Grande Armée stragglers

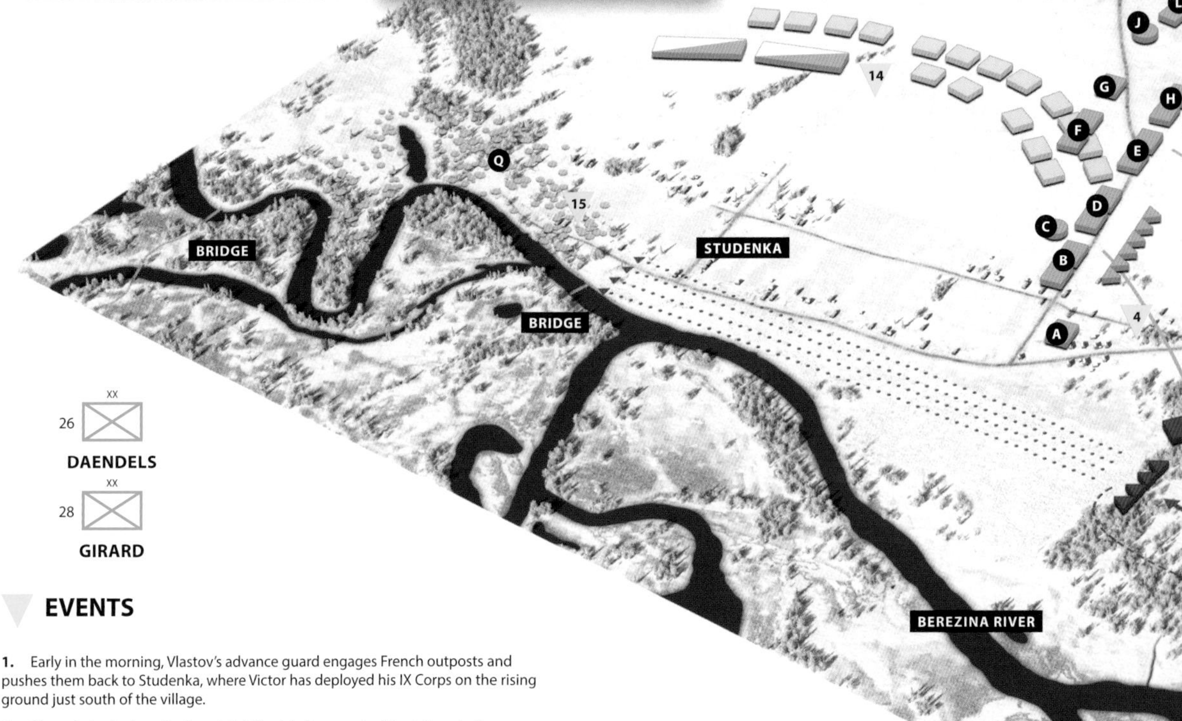

EVENTS

1. Early in the morning, Vlastov's advance guard engages French outposts and pushes them back to Studenka, where Victor has deployed his IX Corps on the rising ground just south of the village.

2. Cossacks try to turn the French left flank but are pushed back Fournier's cavalrymen.

3. Vlastov moves the 23rd Jägers to secure the small patch of woods bordering the river and to threaten Victor's right flank. A 12-cannon battery (from 1st Horse Artillery Company and 28th Battery Company) starts to bombard the crowds near the bridges, spreading chaos.

4. With the support of a strong French battery on the western shore, the Badenese Brigade drives the Russians back and secures the woods.

5. Vlastov deploys artillery to bombard Victor's positions.

6. Victor orders the Berg Brigade to attack Vlastov's position on the main road.

7. The timely arrival of Russian Lieutenant-General Berg's forces allows the Russians to repel the enemy attack. The 24th Jägers engage the Berg units while the remaining Russian regiments deploy on the right side of the road. The French attack is repelled.

8. By noon, Fock's units arrive and take up positions on the right side of the main road.

9. The Nizovskii and Voronezhskii Infantry Regiment attack the French centre and threaten to penetrate it.

10. Victor moves forward part of Girard's Polish division and orders Fournier to charge with his cavalry to blunt the Russian assault and gain precious time.

11. Launching 'The Charge of Death', Fournier's Badenese and Hessians slow the Russian attack, but suffer heavy losses.

12. Encouraged by Fournier's attack, Girard's Polish troops, supported by Saxons, charge and push the Russians back.

13. To contain the enemy advance, Fock commits his grenadier battalions; The Combined Cuirassier Regiment and Mogilevskii Infantry Regiment support the attack, seeking to envelop the French flank.

14. Unable to contain the Russian counter-attack, Victor is forced to pull back his units and make a stand near the bridges. Nightfall brings an end to the fighting.

15. Late in the evening, Victor receives orders to cross the river. The remaining crowds are allowed to cross during the night. Around 9am the following morning, the bridges are destroyed.

THE BEREZINA: EAST OF THE RIVER, 28–29 NOVEMBER

Marshal Claude Victor-Perrin's IX Corps was tasked with covering the final phase of the Grande Armée's river crossing. Despite facing the numerically superior Russian forces, Victor's men – an amalgam of the French, Berg, Badenese, Polish, and Saxon troops – held their ground for most of the day before making an orderly retreat across the river and burning the bridges to halt the Russian pursuit.

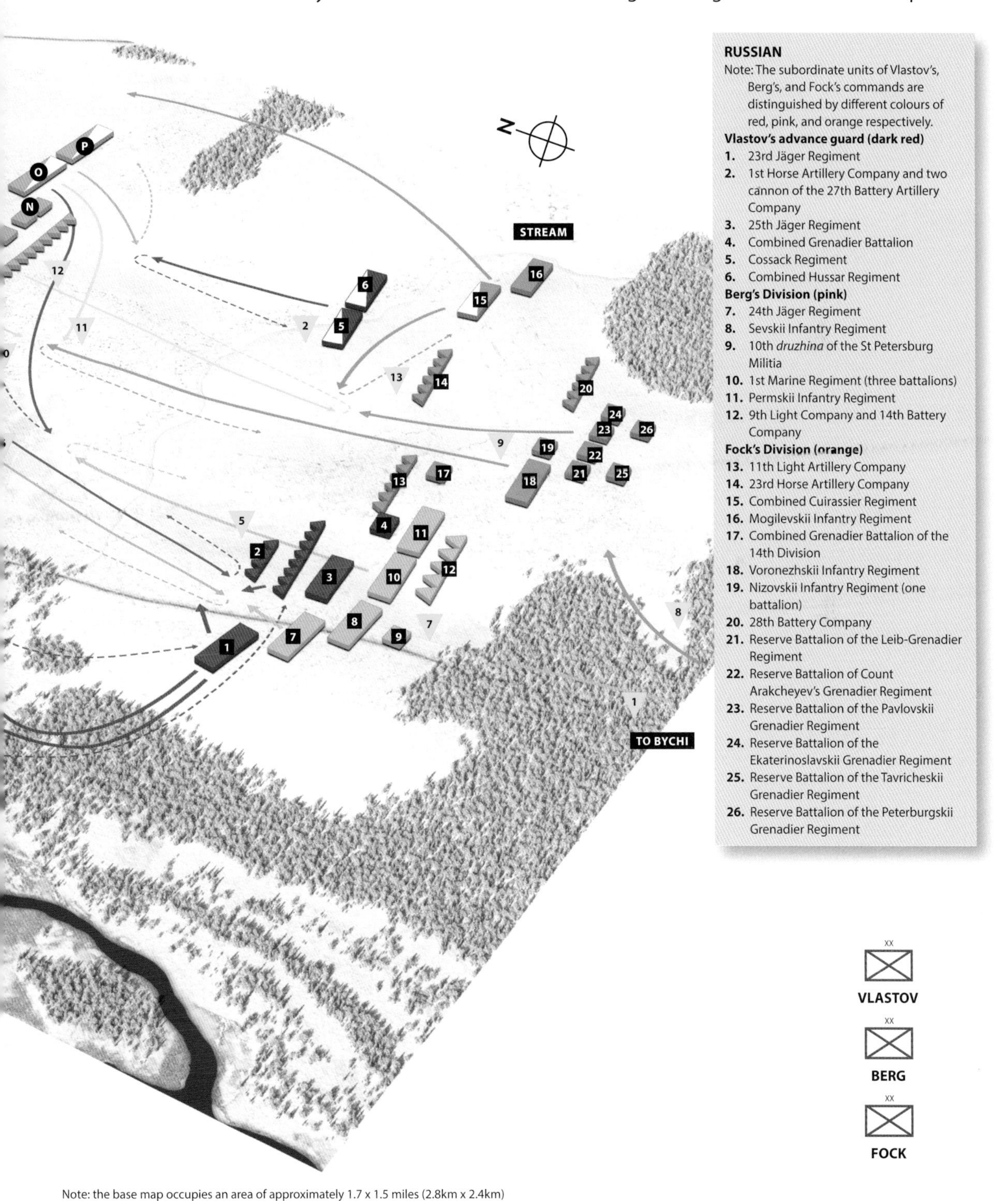

Note: the base map occupies an area of approximately 1.7 x 1.5 miles (2.8km x 2.4km)

the French position. Victor and his men demonstrated the necessary *sang froid* and presence of mind. The marshal moved forward part of Girard's Polish division and ordered Fournier to charge with his cavalry to blunt the Russian assault and gain precious time. Amidst the murderous crossfire, the Badenese hussars and the Hessian Chevau-légers did what was expected of them – galloping down the hillsides, they crashed into the Russian infantry and rolled it backward. 'The Charge of Death', as this remarkable exploit became known, halted the Russian advance but at a grievous price; both these fine cavalry regiments were destroyed and barely 50 Badenese and two dozen Hessians survived to see the morrow. Still, their sacrifice allowed the rest of Girard's Polish division, supported by Saxon troops, to execute a fierce counter-attack that came close to piercing the Russian centre, when the Russian generals sent in reinforcements and restored the conflict. The Poles suffered grievously from the canister fire and were mauled by the joint attack of the Combined Cuirassier Regiment and the replacement battalions of the 1st Grenadier Division. Equally successful was the counter-attack of the Combined Cuirassier Regiment and the Mogilevskii Infantry Regiment, which threatened to envelop the French left flank and forced Victor to pull back his units hastily and make a desperate stand near the bridges.

The Russian generals could sense victory and were rallying their men for one final push that would overwhelm their opponent. 'I was already about to send out my adjutants to convey the order to all my battalion columns,' remembered Lieutenant-General Berg, 'when General Diebitsch arrived with the orders from Count Wittgenstein. He asked me, "What are you planning to do?" and, upon me explaining my intention, he told me, "On behalf of the count, I order you to stop this assault."' The general argued further attacks were futile and nothing more could be achieved. Berg was dumbfounded. 'I could not defy the count but this incident only further underscored how much the enemy was still feared. We knew that Napoleon was still with the army and he was feared like the lion that no beast dares to approach.' The attack was called off, and for the rest of that evening the Russians limited their attacks to skirmishing and artillery fire.

The nightfall brought an end to these scenes of carnage and confusion. Rafail Zotov, an ensign in the St Petersburg Militia, watched as the Russian artillery continued to fire at the tottering masses thronging the riverbank. 'In front of them stood a few French columns that repelled with remarkable bravery all our attempts to reach the crossing site.' That evening, Victor despondently reported that 'many soldiers and officers have been killed or wounded'. His corps lost over 4,000 men, almost two-thirds of its strength, and some regiments were reduced to battalion strengths. The officer corps was decimated; Victor himself suffered a contusion, Daendels was bruised after falling off his horse, and generals Damas, Geither, Lingg, Girard and Fournier were all wounded. The Russian casualties were equally grave, at about 4,000 men.

Wittgenstein's actions during the battle at Studenka remain puzzling. He stayed away from the battlefield, acted half-heartedly and failed to utilize his numerical superiority; just half of his troops took part in the battle, a high number of which were newly raised militiamen. Furthermore, as the battle wound down, the general informed Chichagov of his intention to stop the pursuit due to heavy losses and fatigue. Once again, the admiral was left alone to contend with Napoleon.

The pursuit, 29 November–2 December 1812

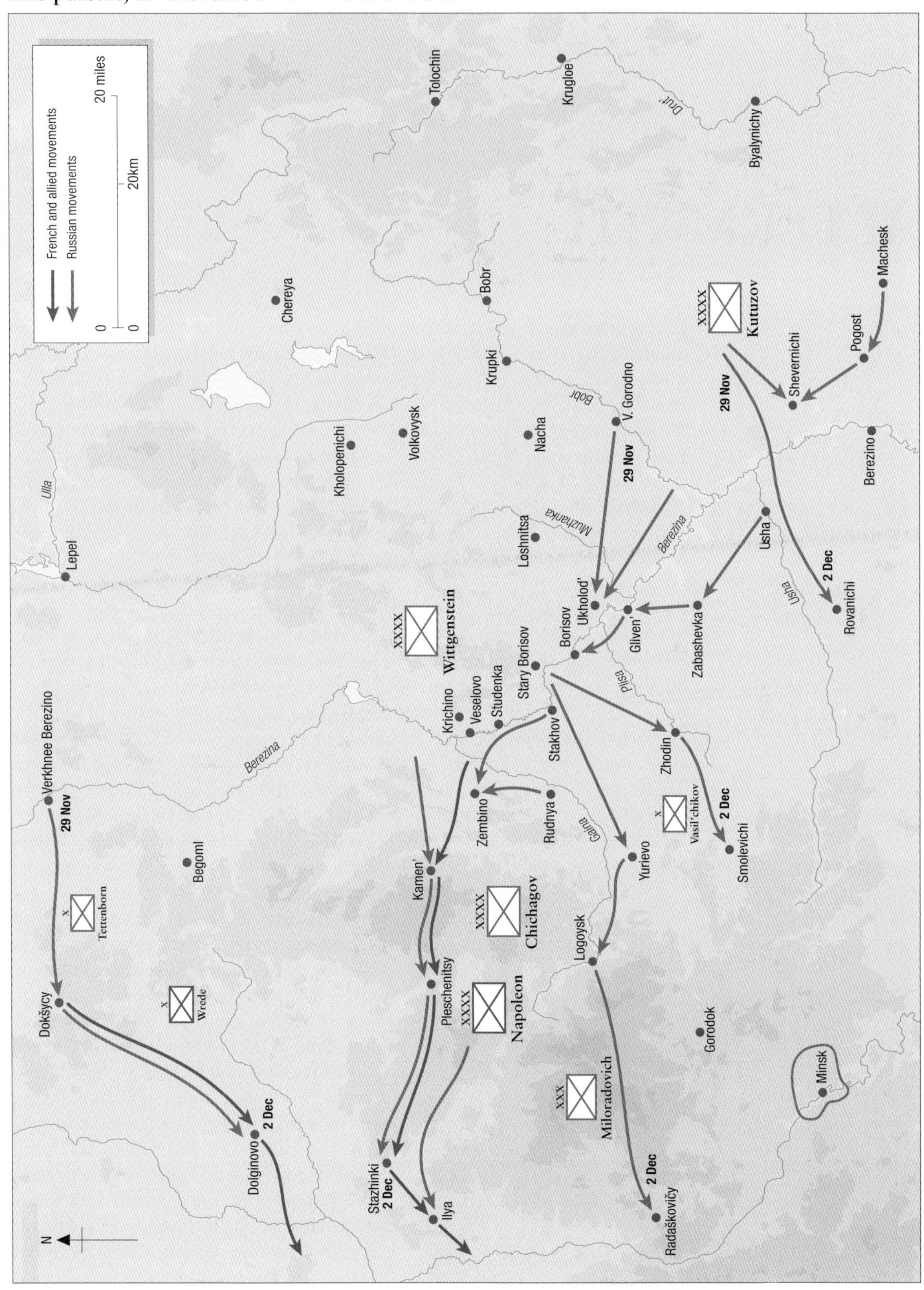

AFTERMATH

Late in the evening, Victor received orders to cross the river. Eblé and his engineers had to cut a swathe through the ghastly pile up of broken vehicles and corpses so that the remnants of the IX Corps could pass. It was well after midnight when the last of them was finally across. Eblé did his best to move as many stragglers as he could over the bridges, but many became torpid with despair and would not move; 'we no longer knew how to appreciate danger and we did not even have enough energy to fear it,' commented a French colonel. Eblé's orders were to destroy the crossings at 8am, but he waited beyond the set hour hoping to save some more lives. At long last, around 9am, he could wait no more and fired the bridges.

The final act of the Berezina tragedy then unfolded as the crowd, as if awakened from slumber, realized what was happening and dashed to the bridges in search of salvation. It was too late. Some attempted to run through the flames and died trying. Others endeavoured to swim across – 'I saw them all in the water up to their shoulders,' remembered Bourgogne. 'Overcome by the terrible cold, they all perished.' Later that morning, the cry went up, 'The Cossacks are coming!' They did indeed, ruthlessly plundering and pilfering the survivors while the Grande Armée watched helplessly from across the river. The scene reminded one eyewitness of the Acheron, the underworld river of the Greek myths: 'The damned were on the left bank; the elect on the right.'

Napoleon and his troops during the retreat. (Fine Art Images/ Heritage Images/Getty Images)

The Russian participants were deeply shaken by what they saw on that riverbank. 'never have I experienced the senses of horror as I did that day,' General Berg noted. For Rochechouart, 'there could be nothing sadder, more distressing' than seeing countless heaps of dead men, women and children, 'of soldiers of every formation, of every nation, frozen, crushed by the fugitives or struck down by Russian grapeshot'. It was impossible to conceive a more terrifying sight than that of two broken bridges and the frozen river full of the dead. Martos could never forget a woman whom he found half-frozen in the ice. 'One of her arms had been hacked off and hung only by a vein, while the other held a baby which had wrapped its arms

A huge column of French and allied soldiers trudges through the desolate Russian landscape. This painting by Nicolas Toussaint Charlet (1792–1845) highlights the suffering of the individual soldiers. (Leemage/Corbis via Getty Images)

around its mother's neck. The woman was still alive and her expressive eyes were fixed on a man who had fallen beside her, and who had already frozen to death. Between them, on the ice, lay their dead child.' And what made the scene even more bewildering was the vast number of carriages overloaded with the immeasurable booty that the Grande Armée had taken in the Russian towns and cities. There were magnificent carriages, berlines, calashes, phaetons, drozhkys and other transports laden with rich jewellery, luxurious furs, sacred gold goblets and religious vestments from the churches of Moscow, paintings, engravings, countless books, silver dishes and porcelain. 'Many a man partook in these immense riches,' admitted one Russian general. 'Everyone took what had not been yet claimed and what he could carry away. The whole area resembled a disturbed ant-hill where each and every ant drags away its own egg or straw.' From generals to common soldiers, everyone partook in the sharing of the spoils. 'Vlastov showed me a purse full of ducats and louis d'ors, and also a beautiful carriage that he had claimed,' remembered Lieutenant-General Berg.

The loss of life at the Berezina will never be exactly known. The Grande Armée lost between 25,000 and 40,000 men, the vast majority of them stragglers and non-combatants. Regiments that had kept up their discipline and organization throughout the retreat were decimated and only a few thousand, probably no more than 9,000 men, mainly Poles and the veterans of the Imperial Guard, were in any state to bear arms. The II Corps lost half of its effective strength, the IX Corps two-thirds; three days after the crossing, Ney reported that the Vistula Legion counted only 200 men, the 16th Polish Division 190 men, and the 18th Division 133 men. The officer corps was devastated; some 1,600 officers were killed and wounded and hundreds more captured. Thirty-one generals became casualties, one of the highest senior officer losses of the entire Napoleonic Wars; for comparison, 23 generals were lost at Eylau, 49 at Borodino, and 35 at Waterloo. Wittgenstein reported that in the wake of the battles on the Berezina his corps captured five enemy generals, five colonels, 16 lieutenant-colonels, 290 officers, and 10,800 soldiers along with over a dozen cannon. Chichagov's after-action report,

Napoleon leaves the Grande Armée at Smorgoni (modern Smarhoń) to return to Paris. (Chronicle/Alamy)

meanwhile, spoke of 52 officers and over 5,200 men captured. Four days after the crossing, the main Russian army's official *Journal of the Military Operations* recorded the capture of 432 officers and 23,500 enemy soldiers, along with 22 cannons and four colours. The loss of life among these prisoners was enormous, and many of them perished from illness, hunger, cold and mistreatment in the days to come.

Napoleon's retreat from the Berezina offers little of military interest. The Grande Armée had effectively ceased to exist as a fighting force, and a mass of fugitives trailed mechanically along the route west, in the words of Napoleon, 'like vagabonds or rather like brigands'. Captain Coignet lamented the collapse of discipline and 'any human feeling for one another; each man looked out for himself'. The weather deteriorated and the infamous Russian frost wrought havoc on the survivors. 'The sky showed a still more dreadful appearance,' remembered Ségur. 'The air was motionless and silent: it seemed as if everything which possessed life and movement in nature – the wind itself – had been seized, chained, and as it were, frozen by a universal death.' Eyewitnesses described the corpses of men and horses, along with abandoned guns and vehicles, strewn as far as the eye could see. The burned-out remains of the villages were scenes of utter human degradation.

Napoleon considered his job as a military leader largely done. 'In this state of affairs I think my presence in Paris necessary for France, for the empire, for the wellbeing of the army itself,' he reasoned on 29 November. Six days later, he left the army and returned to France to prepare for the new campaign. The unhappy victims of his overweening ambition plodded forward to Vilna, where they found only more desolation and death. By the end of December, the last of the Grande Armée soldiers had crossed the Niemen River. The Russian campaign was over.

Much has been written about the battle of the Berezina and the Russian campaign. The news of the disaster, revealed in Napoleon's infamous 29th Bulletin, filled French minds with fear and gloomy foreboding. The very name of the river where the Grande Armée suffered such heavy losses became synonymous with a terrible and irreparable disaster. Yet the crossing of the Berezina also became a symbol of heroism, endurance, perseverance, and selfless sacrifice. Over the years, it was shrouded with a certain aura that inspired writers and poets to pick up their quills. Honoré de Balzac devoted one of his best short stories to the crossing and Victor Hugo evoked the heroic images in his famous *Châtiments*. French novelist Henry Murger confidently proclaimed that 'Caesar crossed the Rubicon but he would not have made it beyond the Berezina'. For contemporaries, Berezina was one of the most spectacular moments in an era full of drama and excitement. They struggled to name another example where an army, facing desperate circumstances, suffering from cold, famine and exhaustion, surrounded by the enemy armies and pressed against a river, had extricated itself more skilfully. For Guillaume-

Joseph Roux, Baron Peyrusse, this was nothing short of 'a phenomenon', while many shared Baron Henri de Jomini's conclusion that 'the celebrated passage of the Berezina is one of the most remarkable operations in history'.

Historians have long praised Napoleon for his leadership and ascribed the Grande Armée's escape to the brilliance of his military genius, which sprang to action in this desperate crisis and hoodwinked his opponents. But a closer examination of the facts leads to a more circumspect appreciation of the French emperor's accomplishment. We may certainly agree with a French historian's assessment that Berezina was '*une victoire militaire*', but only inasmuch as to mean that the remnants of the army were saved as a result of the enemy commanders badly mishandling the situation. Napoleon did act quickly and with his customary flexibility, yet the crossing of the Berezina was not the result of his fertile military genius but of a combination of factors, including capable leadership at the divisional and regimental level of the Grande Armée, the incredible heroism of the rank and file, especially the engineers and pontonniers and, most crucially, the mismanagement of the situation by the Russian military leaders.

Debate over who was responsible for Napoleon's escape began almost as soon as the battle on the Berezina ended. 'At nightfall, everything calmed down,' wrote Zotov, a soldier in Wittgenstein's corps. 'Our entire corps gathered around bivouacs and, as bonfires ignited, reflections, debates, and speculations poured out at once.' What did the events of the day mean? How and why was Napoleon allowed to cross? Why was he even allowed to build the bridges? Why had Chichagov's army not trampled him back into the river when the crossing began? Why did not Kutuzov follow on Napoleon's heels to destroy him on the riverbank? 'These thoughts kept us guessing all night long,' Zotov commented. 'We deplored Chichagov first, then Kutuzov, and finally even our own Wittgenstein. The whole Berezina affair seemed to us pathetic and suspicious.'

Kutuzov learned of Napoleon's escape en route to the Berezina. 'He was very upset,' remembered a staff officer. Trying to understand what had transpired there, he solicited documents and questioned various officers.

Marshal Michel Ney leading the rear guard out of Russia, a painting by Adolph Yvon. Ney was reputedly among the last of Napoleon's troops to leave Russia. (The Print Collector/Alamy)

Chichagov and Wittgenstein both committed their share of 'grave mistakes', he concluded, conveniently forgetting that his own unenergetic pursuit, as one participant put it, 'gave the French complete freedom to flee'. Still, the field marshal was upset that Chichagov had not reached Borisov earlier and did not take better precautions to guard against enemy diversions; he was particularly upset that, contrary to his earlier instructions, the wooden causeways through the Zembino marshes were not destroyed. Kutuzov was also critical of Wittgenstein who, despite the strength of his corps, made no attempt to press the enemy hard and acted so cautiously during those crucial days. 'We should not be surprised by his restraint,' one Russian military historian ruefully observed, for Wittgenstein 'did not want to imperil the fame he had acquired with earlier victories.' Sardinian ambassador Joseph de Maistre reflected what many in Russian society thought that winter when he pointed out that Wittgenstein, in his subsequent report, spoke of 'forcing' the enemy to cross the river, which meant that he was in fact undercutting Chichagov, whose mission was to prevent such a crossing in the first place.

With the army and the public demanding a scapegoat for Napoleon's escape, Chichagov became a convenient target. Kutuzov and Wittgenstein were unassailable public figures, eulogized and extolled as national heroes; the former was credited with saving the whole of Russia and extolled as 'the conqueror of the world-conqueror'; the latter was hailed as the saviour of St Petersburg. It would have been impossible to criticize them, especially when those in the know, like Lieutenant-General Berg, chose to remain silent. By contrast, Chichagov lacked the gravitas of Kutuzov and the popularity of Wittgenstein. His impetuosity and brash treatment of subordinates, commented Tyrconnell, meant that even his own officers had no desire to stand up for 'their commander who mistreats them, shows indecisiveness in planning, and always blames his mistakes on them'. When Lieutenant-General Berg met his brother, Burghardt von Berg, who served as the quartermaster-general of the Third Western Army, he was surprised to hear him lambasting the admiral for mishandling the situation. The Russian army and society were soon saturated with stories of Chichagov's incompetence. 'Our *admiral* [original emphasis] has scattered all our advantages to the winds,' lamented one senior officer, while Maistre could not find anyone in St Petersburg who did not condemn Chichagov as 'an abominable traitor'.

Condemned, ridiculed and ostracized, Chichagov left the army for 'health' reasons but privately he confided that it was 'due to Kutuzov's endless fault-finding'. He endured the popular anger 'with his usual dignity, honour, and firmness' (as de Maistre saw it) refusing to be drawn into a public confrontation with the field marshal. Behind the scenes he tried his best to justify his actions and to induce the emperor into defending him; but Alexander refused to go against public opinion, especially if it would require him to strike down 'the nation's idol' Kutuzov. 'The crowd is blind,' grumbled Chichagov. 'It can be easily deceived and manipulated. But what should we think about those who, despite knowing the truth, still tolerate falsehoods and slander?' Hounded relentlessly by the public, the admiral left Russia and spent the rest of his life in England, where he wrote his memoirs in an unsuccessful bid to clear his name. He outlived Kutuzov and Napoleon, but the last decades of his life were full of melancholy and frustration as he watched his great rivals extolled and lionized, while popular opinion still held him responsible for what had happened on the Berezina.

THE BATTLEFIELD TODAY

The Berezina battlefield is relatively well preserved. The town of Borisov (present-day Barysaw) and neighbouring settlements have grown in size, but the crossing site remains relatively unaffected by the urban sprawl. The area is easily accessible by car using the P53 motorway that spans the 45 miles that separate the Belarusian capital Minsk from Borisov, where visitors can pay a quick visit to the remnants of the famed tête-de-pont, examine some of its surviving ramparts, and walk through the little park that surrounds them. They can then take an exit to the P63 motorway that runs along the eastern bank to Bychi/Bytcha and Studenka and then, crossing the river, to Zembino; to explore the battlefield on the western side of the river, visitors should follow the H8114 road that runs from Borisov to Bryli/Brili.

The Berezina battlefields are dotted with various monuments. Attempts to commemorate the battle began with Emperor Nicholas I's decision to erect two wooden posts, with the carved letter N (in Russian, H), to mark the entrances to the long-gone bridges at Studenka. Some, however, questioned the validity of their placement. Ivan Kolodeyev (1859–1914), a local resident who had devoted his entire life to studying the Berezina crossing and amassed one of the largest Napoleonic collections in the Russian Empire, thought that the posts were wrongly placed. In November 1901, he constructed red granite monuments at what he concluded were the actual locations of the bridges. These monuments showed haut-reliefs of Alexander and Napoleon

A monument erected at the site of the second bridge crossing over the Berezina River. (Alain Poirot/Alamy)

The granite obelisk dedicated to fallen Russian Jäger troops at the Berezina River. Built in 1912, it was destroyed in the Soviet era and rebuilt in 1992. The honour guard includes modern-day Russian Jäger reenactors. (Alain Poirot/Alamy)

on the eastern and western sides, and inscriptions – 'Here Emperor Napoleon crossed the Berezina with his army on 14–16 November 1812' – in Russian and French on the southern and northern sides. The memorials suffered during the political and social turmoil that engulfed Russia in the 20th century; they were seriously damaged during the Civil War and World War II, and demolished in 1962; one of them was, however, restored for the 190th anniversary of the battle in 2002.

The centennial anniversary of the Berezina brought new monuments, the best of them being the tall granite obelisk dedicated to the soldiers and officers of the Russian 7th, 10th and 12th Jäger regiments. Designed by Captain Ivan Demyakov, it was unveiled in May 1913 but, like Kolodeyev's memorial, suffered great damage in the subsequent decades. Destroyed during the Soviet–Polish War of 1920, it was rebuilt by the Belarusian authorities on the 180th anniversary of the crossing in November 1992.

During World War II, when the German Army occupied Borisov, the 1st Battalion of the 638th Regiment of the French Volunteer Legion (*Légion des Voluntaires Français contre le Bolshevisme*) paid respect to the French soldiers who fought on the Berezina by building a 8ft-tall brick monument to commemorate the 130th anniversary of the battle in 1942; the memorial was demolished when Soviet troops liberated the town.

In 1962, in commemoration of the 150th anniversary of the battle, the Soviet authorities built three memorials. A rough stone slab was erected where one of Kolodeyev's original monuments had identified the entrance to the infantry bridge on the eastern bank. Its plaque simply declares: 'Here, on the Berezina, the Russian army under M.I. Kutuzov completed the destruction of the Napoleonic forces on 14–16 (26–28) November 1812. The memory of the heroic exploits of the peoples of Russia, who defended the honour and independence of their land, will always live.'

The second monument, built at the 10-mile marker on the motorway from Borisov to Zembino, is a stele with a white marble plaque that is inscribed: 'Here, the Russian army routed the retreating forces of the French Emperor Napoleon during the crossing of the Berezina on 14–16 (26–28) November 1812.'

The third, and largest memorial, designed by N. Ryzhenkov, is the massive black stone slab with a relief of the Russian forces on one side and the following inscription on the other: 'During the Napoleonic Army's crossing of the Berezina River on 26–28/14–16 November 1812, Russian forces completed the destruction of the remnants of the Napoleonic aggressors in the battles at Borisov, Studenka, and Stakhov'.

The most poignant of the Berezina monuments is the so-called 'Swiss memorial' (see p. 78) to the victims of the tragic events on the Berezina. Sculpted by A. Artimovich and funded by the Swiss Foreign Ministry, this memorial shows a youthful hero breathing his last under the shadow of a flag held up by a mighty eagle; the curving shapes of the massive stone slab, on which the figure rests, evoke the icy waves of the Berezina where so many found their final peace.

In 1997, another memorial was opened on the Bryli field as the result of the steadfast efforts of French historian Fernand Beacour and the Centre d'études napoléoniennes (Paris). The granite monument carries a bronze plaque with an inscription in Belarusian and French: 'Here, Napoleon's army had crossed the Berezina on 26–29 November. In Memory of Soldiers who Perished.'

Grande Armée reenactors carry a coffin containing the remains of a French soldier killed in 1812 during the reburial ceremony of 220 soldiers in Bryli, in November 2007. (VIKTOR DRACHEV/AFP via Getty Images)

FURTHER READING

Adam, A. (trans. J. North), *Napoleon's Army in Russia: The Illustrated Memoirs of Albrecht Adam*, Barnsley: Pen & Sword, 2005

Arkhiv Admirala P.V. Chichagova, St Petersburg, 1885

Austin, Paul Britten, *1812: The Great Retreat*, London: Greenhill Books, 1996

Beaucour, Fernand Emile et al, *La Bérézina: Une Victoire Militaire*, Paris, 2006

Benthien, George Diederich (ed. J. Eysten), 'Doorloopend Verhaal van de Dienstverrichtingen der Nederlandsche Pontonniers onder den Majoor G.D. Benthien 1797–1825', in *Bijdragen en Mededeelingen van het Historisch Genootschap*, XXXII (1911), pp. 100–177

Berg, Gregor von, *Autobiographie des Generalen der Infanterie Gregor von Berg*, Dresden: E. Blochman, 1871

Beskrovnyi, Liubomir (ed.), *M.I. Kutuzov: Sbornik Dokumentov*, Volume 4, Moscow, 1954

Bielecki, Robert, *Berezyna 1812*, Warsaw, 1990

Bogdanovich, Modest, *Istoria Otechestvennoi Voiny 1812 g. po Dostovernym Istochnikam*, Volume 3, St Petersburg, 1859

Cappello, Girolamo, *Gli Italiani in Russia nel 1812*, Città di Castello, 1912

Chichagov, Pavel, *Mémoires de l'amiral Tchitchagoff (1767–1849)*, Leipzig, 1862

Fabry, Gabriel-Joseph, *Campaign de 1812: Documents Relatifs à l'Aile Gauche, 20 Août – 4 Décembre*, Paris, 1912

Kharkevich, V., *1812 g. Berezina*, St Petersburg, 1893

Küpfer, Emile,. *Nos Dernières Pages d'Histoire Héroique: La Suisse à Polotzk et à la Bérésina*, Lausanne, 1912

Lalowski, Marek Tadeusz and North, Jonathan (eds), *Polish Eyewitnesses to Napoleon's 1812 Campaign*, Barnsley: Pen & Sword, 2020

Mikaberidze, Alexander, *Napoleon's Great Escape: The Battle of the Berezina*, Barnsley: Pen & Sword, 2010

Muralt, Albrecht von, and Legler, Thomas, *Beresina: Erinnerungen aus dem Feldzug Napoleons I in Russland 1812*, Bern, 1940

Partouneaux, Louis, *Adresse du Lieutenant-Général Partouneaux à l'Armée Française et Rapports sur l'Affaire du 27 au 28 Novembre 1812*, Paris, 1815

Vasiliyev, I., *Neskolko Gromkikh Udarov po Khvostu Tigra*, Moscow, 2001

Vaudoncourt, Frédéric-François Guillaume de, *Relation Impartiale du Passage de la Berezina, par l'Armée Française, en 1812*, Paris, 1815

Vlijmen, B.R.F. van, *Vers la Bérésina (1812) d'après des Documents Nouveaux*, Paris, 1908

INDEX

Figures in **bold** refer to illustrations.